# WALKING THROUGH EDEN

# WALKING THROUGH EDEN

## A RIVERSIDE JOURNEY

## NEIL HANSON

PAVILION

First published in 1990 by
PAVILION BOOKS LIMITED
196 Shaftesbury Avenue, London WC2H 8JL

Designed by Tom Sawyer

A CIP catalogue record for this book
is available from the British Library

ISBN 1-85145-393-8

10 9 8 7 6 5 4 3 2 1

Printed and bound in Great Britain by
Billing & Sons Limited, Worcester
Typeset by Wyvern Typesetting Ltd, Bristol.

# CONTENTS

St Mary's, Mallerstang

# $\mathcal{A}$CKNOWLEDGEMENTS

MANY PEOPLE GAVE FREELY OF their time and knowledge during my research for this book. I have drawn extensively on the characters, attitudes and opinions of the many men and women that I met while walking through Eden and during my frequent pauses at the pubs along the way.

In order to spare their blushes and save them from possibly unwelcome intrusions, however, I have changed their names. You will find no Ben Alderson or Michael Parker living in Eden, for example, though you may encounter their originals walking along a lane by the river. Friends and acquaintances will no doubt recognize some characters despite their camouflage; I rely on their discretion to leave the real Ben Alderson and his peers in peace.

I have also sometimes merged two or more characters to form a whole. Students of Trades Union Conferences will know that 'compositing' is an honourable tradition, and where two separate farmers, for example, have expressed views of a similar tenor, I have occasionally taken the liberty of allowing their opinions to issue from a single mouth. As well as these anonymous benefactors, my thanks also to Keith and Ann, for their many kindnesses to me.

Many people outside Defoe's 'wall of brass' also helped to keep me clear of the rocks on my way down the Eden. I am grateful to my publisher Colin Webb, to my copy editor, Steve

# ACKNOWLEDGEMENTS

Dobell, and all the staff at Pavilion Books, in particular, my desk editor Joanne Rippin.

Finally, my special thanks to Viv Bowler, whose enthusiasm and encouragement were instrumental in launching me on the Eden, and to Mark Lucas, a friend and wise counsellor as well as my agent, whose insights and criticisms on the early drafts of the text were invariably accurate and, as befits a good agent, always tactfully phrased.

Quotations used in the text have been taken from the following sources:

*Britannica*, Camden (p. 35 & 105);
*Tour Through the Whole Island of Great Britain*, Daniel Defoe (p. 9);
*History and Antiquities of Cumberland and Westmorland*, Nicolson & Burn (p. 69 & 155);
*English Fairs and Markets*, William Addison, Pub. Batsford Ltd (p. 76)
*Oxford Book of Ballads*, ed Quiller-Couch (p. 180);
*Tour to Alston Moor*, Thomas Pennant (p. 143);
*Chronicle of Lanercost*, ed H. Maxwell (p. 179);
*Two Drovers*, Sir Walter Scott (p. 76);
*St Ives*, R. L. Stevenson (p. 76);
*The Prelude*, William Wordsworth (p. 148 & 166);
*Scoop*, Evelyn Waugh, reprinted by permission of the Peters Fraser & Dunlop Group Ltd (p. 33);
*The London Daily News* (p. 46 & 62);
*A Review of Reports to the Board of Agriculture for the Northern Department of England (1808)*, William Marshall (p. 40);
*Six Month Tour Through the North of England*, Arthur Young (p. 69);
*Description of the County of Westmoreland*, Daniel Fleming (p. 69);
*The Ruin of Britain*, Gildas, trans. P. Winterbottom (p. 179).

# ·EDEN·

'*HERE we entered Westmore-land, a country eminent only for being the wildest, most barren and frightful of any that I have passed over in England, or even in Wales it self; the west side which borders on Cumberland, is indeed bounded of almost unpassable mountains, which, in the language of the country are called Fells. . . and the English Apennine, that is, the mountains of Yorkshire North Riding, lie like a wall of brass on the other. . . The River Eden, rises in this part out of the side of a monstrous high mountain, called Mowill Hill, or Wildbore Fell, which you please; after which, it runs through the middle of this vale, which is. . . a very agreeable and pleasant country, or perhaps seems to be so the more, by the horror of the eastern and southern part.*'

Daniel Defoe

*A Tour Through the Whole Island of Great Britain*

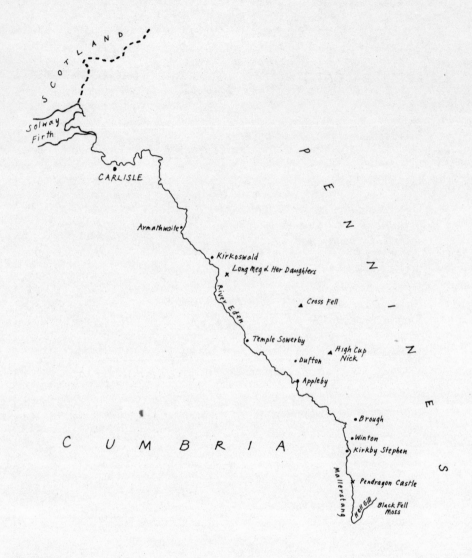

SCOTLAND

Solway
Firth

• CARLISLE

P
E
N
N
I
N
E
S

Armathwaite•

• Kirkoswald
✕ Long Meg & Her Daughters

River Eden

▲ Cross Fell

• Temple Sowerby

• Dufton

High Cup
Nick ▲

• Appleby

• Brough

• Winton

✕ Kirkby Stephen

CUMBRIA

Mallerstang

✕ Pendragon Castle

Hell Gill

Black Fell
Moss

# INTRODUCTION

The River Eden

lonely, wind-swept inn, seventeen hundred feet above sea
level in the high Pennines, set alone in an ocean of peat bog and
heather moorland that stretched away, unbroken, as far as the
eye could see.

Winter hung on grimly up there, long after it had released
its grip on the lowlands, and it returned far earlier, the brief
summer greening of the moors reverting swiftly to a dull,
barren brown.

Almost every morning of those two years, I would drive
the winding, single-track road over the moors to the west.
Always the wind was blowing and often the cloud was down or
rain or snow were driving across the fells, shrouding the land
from view, but when the cloud lifted and the sun broke
through, the quartz crystals in the road surface sparkled like a
million diamonds.

On such days, I would stop when I reached the scarp at
the edge of the moor and gaze out over the green, beautiful
strand of the Eden Valley laid out below me, following the
river's sinuous course as it snaked away far to the north. To look
down from the cold, bleak wilderness of the tops to that lush
vision of fertility, was to appreciate how apt was the name of
Eden, in Wordsworth's phrase 'A name fetched from paradise
and rightfully borne.'

Then I drove on down into the valley, a gentler, softer
place, where the cutting edge of the wind was dulled and the
day warmer. On my return, I would pause again at the moor
edge, looking back over my shoulder for a last sight of Eden,
before driving on over the cold and lonely fells. I resolved then

that one day I would follow the river from high in those sour, sombre moors, to its end far away, where the sun glinted on the waters of the Solway.

I would begin my journey in the dead of winter, at the source of the river on Black Fell Moss, and return to Eden throughout the year. From the High Way in Mallerstang to the ancient ford across the Solway Firth, I would walk the old tracks through Eden, travelling the river with the seasons, to reach the Solway in winter once more.

At first glance there is little to link the upland farmers at Eden's head with the salmon haaf-netters of the Solway, let alone the city-dwellers of Carlisle, but the river is a thread binding together those disparate communities, through the endless cycle as the Eden waters gather in the fells and flow down to the sea, to be reborn as rain falling again on those high hills. The gift of rain exacts a tribute, for the Eden carries away rock and earth, the mountains slowly moving to the sea; but the wheel turns, for each loss there is a gain.

The river's cycle is mirrored in the constant exchange between the hills and the Solway shore. Salmon hatch in Eden's upper reaches, then are lost to the sea, but they return years later, to spawn in the place where their life begins and ends. Curlews nest in the uplands, then follow the river to its end, spending the winter, the dead time, probing the soft Solway mud with their moon-sliver beaks, before returning to the fells with the spring. Some of the sheep grazing the fells around the stone pillar which marks Eden's source, spend their first winter cropping the sweet Solway turf by Edward I's cold, stone monument, at the end of Eden.

Even the upland people feel and respond to the pull of the river. Like a busy road or an airport, its mere presence and its constant flow are a reminder that there exists a wider world outside the encircling wall of the hills. Many follow the Eden down towards the sea, drawn to the opportunities of town and city, but most retrace their steps in their middle or later years, settling back, like the returning curlew, into the fells where they were raised.

While this or any river could stand as metaphor for all rivers, the Eden also offers other resonances. At its source and at its end are stone monuments, two opposite poles. On Black Fell Moss, the river's source is marked by a seventeenth century drystone pillar, erected by Lady Anne Clifford. In her thirty years in Eden, that 'Proud Northern Lady' achieved more for the general good of the inhabitants than anyone before or since. After centuries of raiding and warfare, culminating in the trauma and destruction of the Civil War, the work and the charity that she provided kept many from destitution and even starvation.

At the end of Eden, where the river spills into the Solway Firth, a far grander stone monument, surrounded by a spiked iron fence, marks the death-site of a very different character, Edward I, 'the Hammer of the Scots'. He not only initiated the Hundred Years War against France, but also acted as one of the prime architects of three hundred years of almost continual warfare with Scotland.

He expired at the edge of the Solway in 1307, on his way north for one last assault on the old enemy. The Latin inscription on his monument describes him as the 'greatest English king'. Those inhabitants of Eden blessed with Latin might beg leave to differ: his legacy to their ancestors was three centuries of ceaseless Scots raiding, killing, raping, burning and plundering, which left traces still visible today. Throughout Eden, buildings remain huddled together, as if fearing still the renewed, brutal attentions of marauding Scots, while the country between settlements lies echoingly empty.

The economic pillaging of the region that followed the Industrial Revolution was less dramatic, but its impact has also been long-lasting. It created a brief prosperity in which few of the inhabitants were privileged to share, and its aftermath has left a land stripped of its natural wealth, cast up, like flotsam, on the Solway shore. Even that great symbol of Victorian power and self-belief, the Settle–Carlisle railway, was allowed for years to decay and disintegrate and still faces an uncertain future. This half-forgotten valley on the northern fringe of

England has become as marginal to its declining nation as once it was to the crumbling Roman Empire.

As Joseph Wright's *English Dialect Dictionary* reveals, traces of the region's turbulent history are everywhere, even in the language, for the Cumbrian dialect has 109 words for beating and 67 for a fool, but very few for affection. Eden's troubled past also reveals itself in the lugubrious fatalism of its present inhabitants, as stolid and indifferent to the problems of the world outside, as it has been to theirs. Had Orson Welles' version of *War of the Worlds* been set in Eden and broadcast on BBC Radio Cumbria, it is unlikely to have had quite the same impact on these phlegmatic people as it did on the population of New York.

'Sad weather, Stan.'

'Aye.'

'I see the Martians have landed, then.'

'Aye.'

'Aye. Well. Two more pints of bitter please Doris.'

The same stoicism also seems to characterize the Eden livestock. One bright, early spring morning, I watched a few cows placidly grazing in a riverside pasture, ignoring the rooks standing on their backs and pulling out beakfuls of hair to line their nests. In that same warm, wet spring, I saw sheep similarly unconcerned by grass actually growing out of their fleeces. The farmer had set up a metal hay rack in the field and, while the sheep browsed underneath it for a few stray wisps of hay, seeds dropped from the rack into their fleeces. The wet weather and the warmth of their bodies combined to germinate the seeds and for a couple of days even the sheep greened at the approach of spring, a bizarre symbol of Eden's fertility.

The centuries have inured the human population to far worse misfortunes: Scots raiding and that other implacable scourge of Eden, the weather. If Eskimos have two hundred words for snow, how many more could the inhabitants of the Eden Valley not muster for rain?

As well as discovering Eden, there were things that I wished to discover about myself and the other 'off-comers' drawn irresistibly to this far corner of our overcrowded country. I had felt the need for the stability and community that the uplands offered, both during my time at the inn and in the period of personal turmoil that followed, but what was it that brought so many others here – a rural reality or an urban myth? Why do so many people uproot themselves from their familiar environment and move to remote areas which they can only have experienced superficially, as all tourists do, seeing without knowing? They leave behind their homes, their friends and perhaps a hundred times as many people, clinging to the dream that they, too, may one day do the same. Some day, I would return and search for the answers, walking through Eden.

NEIL HANSON

# 1
# THE PUB ON THE PENNINES

The Pub on the Pennines

pub on the Pennines had been a typically impulsive and quixotic one, taken while living in a state of contented idleness in Holme, a Pennine village, about 75 miles to the south.

I and my wife Sue lived in the village institute. The accommodation was spartan: a stone-flagged living-room, a bedroom, a subterranean kitchen at the bottom of a precipitous flight of steps and a bathroom reached through a large room containing the Institute's pride and joy, a full-sized snooker table. Upstairs, as well as the bathroom, was another large room with a table-tennis table. Our duties as live-in caretakers were less than onerous, for all we had to do was keep the central heating boiler stoked and sweep out the snooker room once a week. Our only other obligation was to pay the scarcely extortionate rent of one pound a week.

Sue had a job some fifteen miles away down the valley, while I was in the early stages of my freelance career; which meant that I spent every morning making myself endless cups of coffee and reading three daily newspapers from cover to cover, including the small advertisements, the court circulars and the births, marriages and deaths. Just when I had finally managed to force myself to think seriously about settling down at the typewriter, the dog would place her chin trustingly on my knee, our dark brown eyes would meet and I would decide to 'just take the dog for a quick walk, before really getting down to work'.

Three hours later, the pair of us would return muddy, tired but exhilarated from a ramble over Black Hill, leaving me just time to towel the dog clean of incriminating mud and peat, crumple a dozen or so sheets of paper and scatter them around my desk and sit down at my typewriter, before Sue returned from her genuinely hard labours, with a solicitous enquiry:

'Had a tough day?'

'Hellish,' I'd reply, getting up to make some coffee and happily abandoning any further attempts at work for the day.

One morning, however, while completing my customary leisurely perusal of the papers, I came across an item in the *Guardian* about the highest pub in England and its owners' search for a new manager. I read the piece with mounting incredulity. The pub was 1,732 feet above sea level, four miles from its next-door neighbour, surrounded by nothing but peat bog and moor, with only sheep and grouse for company. The wind was so strong that it would frequently rip car doors from their hinges, winters were so long and hard that the pub was regularly cut off by snowdrifts for weeks on end and there were no mains services of any sort, just a septic tank for drainage, a geriatric diesel generator for electricity and an arthritic ram pump for water, in a stream four hundred yards from the inn.

'What a preposterous place – only a complete idiot would want to run that,' I thought, dialling directory enquiries. By the time Sue came home that night, I'd arranged an interview. Seven days later, we found ourselves driving up an apparently endless road, cloud down around our ears, rain and wind lashing the surrounding bleak and barren fells.

'We must have missed it,' I said, 'even Heathcliffe wouldn't live up here, let's turn round.'

Since the road was scarcely wide enough for two cars to pass, with glutinous peat bog to either side, we were forced to carry on, and, right at the top of the hill, we found a building even less warm and welcoming than Wuthering Heights. The inn was neither quaint nor attractive: a gaunt stone building covered in cracked and collapsing rendering, painted a hideous, mustard-yellow. To one side was an absurd flat-roofed extension.

Inside, the walls were black with damp and the only light came from candles and storm lanterns, for the generator had broken down. A fire smouldered fitfully in the fireplace, as much smoke entering the room as escaping up the chimney, while from the next room the unmistakable sound of water dripping steadily on to a sodden carpet could be heard.

When we went upstairs to look at the bedroom, I could hear rats scuttling across the ceiling.

'What's that noise?' I asked Neville, one of the owners, a florid-faced Geordie wearing dark glasses, a shiny suit, a kipper tie and enough gold jewellery to finance the national debt of three banana republics.

'Oh, I think a pigeon's got trapped in the loft, I'll pop up and see if I can free it later.'

His smile was broad and friendly, but his eyes, when they could be glimpsed through his sunglasses, were cold and predatory. He was in the scrap trade and looked as straight as a sapling in a force ten gale. As well as his official occupation, he also had his finger in several even more illicit pies.

A few years later, I met him in a Newcastle pub to discuss buying the pub from him. All the time we were talking, he was anxiously looking over his shoulder towards the door.

'It's all right, Neville,' I said, 'It's not illegal to buy and sell pubs.'

'It's not that, I'm waiting for an envelope.'

Five minutes later, the door opened just wide enough to admit a ferret-faced man with lank, unwashed hair and a promising collection of facial blackheads, who appeared to slide rather than walk over to our table. After an appraising look at me, he pulled a bulky brown envelope from inside his jacket, handed it to Neville with a muttered 'Here y'are Nev, it's all there', and was gone. The envelope disappeared into an inside pocket of Neville's capacious camel-hair overcoat and I at last had his undivided attention.

When we had settled on a purchase price for the pub, Neville offered a discount if part was paid in 'poond notes'. I was happy enough with the discount, but dubious of Neville's shady friends and opaque business practices.

'If you want cash, you're going to have to come to my bank to get it,' I told him. 'I'm not walking down the street to find six blokes belting me and running off with the cash and then you coming round the corner, looking innocent and demanding your £15,000.'

Neville gave me a smile as broad as the river Tyne – and as murky – 'I don't know how you could even suggest such a thing, Neil, but if it makes you happy, I'll meet you right outside your bank. I'm not coming in with you, though; I don't want some bank teller pointing me out if questions get asked later on.'

Completion day dawned and, never having held more than £200 in my hands at any one time before, I took along two holdalls to carry the cash. To my disappointment, both were entirely superfluous, for it fitted comfortably into a brown manilla envelope. I went outside to meet Neville, who was once again looking anxiously around while awaiting an envelope. I sat in his beaten-up Volvo, while he licked his thumb and counted the money. Neither candidate requested a recount and, beaming like a returning officer at a by-election when the television lights go on, Neville showed magnanimity in victory.

'You'll be needing some kitchen equipment. Anything you want, I can get you half-price, brand-new.'

'Why, is it stolen?'

'Not yet.'

Neville's partner, Stan, was another Geordie, a civil servant who had far fewer rough edges but who looked, and proved to be, even less trustworthy. He wore a sober, respectable suit and his talk was sweetly reasonable, but his eyes couldn't meet mine for a second, sliding away to focus on the walls, the ceiling or the floor, whenever I tried to hold his gaze. The pair of them reminded me of middle-aged Likely Lads, two kids who grew up in the rough back streets of Newcastle, one staying close to his roots, hustling, wheeling and dealing on the margins, while his best mate got respectable and moved to a new housing estate and a white collar job, without ever quite being able to shake himself free of his Geordie roots.

On the way back down from the inn, Sue and I considered the advantages and disadvantages of accepting the job, if it were offered.

'We'd be giving up a pretty near idyllic existence,' said Sue. 'We'll never get another house for a pound a week.'

'Least of all one with a full-size snooker table.'

'And we're already living in a beautiful place,' she continued, ignoring the interruption. 'It's got moors, hills, lakes, peace and quiet and nice people. I've got a good job and you're just beginning to make a success of freelancing.'

'The local pub isn't bad, either,' I said, helpfully.

'So we've got everything we need where we are,' said Sue. 'We'd have to be mad to want to swap all that for a cold, wet, windy, rat-infested ruin in the middle of nowhere, working for two of the sleaziest people I've ever met.'

'So that settles it, then,' I replied, 'if they offer it we'll take it.'

The result of this *folie à deux* was that three weeks later we were ensconced behind the bar. Neville and Stan gave us a quick Americans-tour-of-Europe guide to running a pub and left us to it. My initiation was short and sharp. On the first evening, I was polishing a glass behind the bar, trying desperately to look like 'mine genial host', when a farmer approached the bar, cap pulled low over his eyes, lower lip jutting out like the prow of a destroyer.

'Dost tha ken Swardle yows?' he demanded.

'Pardon?' I replied.

'Thought so,' he said, stumping off to announce to a group of his peers in the corner that some offcomer with 'plums in his gob' and a total ignorance of Swaledale sheep had taken over the pub.

Despite this unpromising start and the continuing handicaps of my improbable Oxford tones and total inability to tell one sheep from another, the farmers did come to accept and then befriend us, and when you make a friend in the uplands, it's for life. The upland people are shy, reserved and slow to form and voice opinions; there is no question of effusive greetings or invitations to visit on a first acquaintance. If you put on no airs and graces, however, and show yourselves willing to contribute to as well as take from life in the uplands, your reward is friendship and a neighbourliness that has all but disappeared from less stable communities.

Our major contribution to the surrounding communities of Eden, Swaledale and Arkengarthdale was to keep the bar open at hours that would have astonished even the most vehement supporters of licensing law reform, in defiance of fatigue, economics and common sense, although we first had to learn a salutary lesson.

On my first night behind the bar, a Sunday, I thought I would ingratiate myself with the locals with a show of remarkable generosity. The legal closing time of ten-thirty came and went and I said not a word. Eleven passed, eleven-thirty too, and finally, bracing myself for their cries of gratitude and appreciation, I rang the bell and called, 'Time'.

There was a moment's stunned silence, a thunderous roar of laughter, and a cry of 'Just one for the road then,' followed by another burst of laughter as fifty pint pots were presented for refilling.

I learned my lesson fast. From then on we never closed the same day we opened, and we sat up night after night, listening to our locals endlessly debating the merits of particular sheep. Sunday night was the big night, with farmers coming from as much as thirty miles away to talk, drink and argue with ever increasing noise, far into the night.

Except when discussing sheep, the uplander's natural discretion and reticence normally carries over into his conversation, and I found that I had to learn to decode the message underneath. Praise or optimism is sparing. 'All right' denotes complete satisfaction, 'gare [very] good' is the highest praise possible. Uplanders exemplify the old joke about the Northener at a comedy show, who described it as 'All reet, if tha likes laughing'.

Negative feelings are similarly understated. 'Fair to mid-dling' is actually very bad.

'How's your father,' I asked one of our customers, whose father had been ill for some time.

'Oh, he's just fair,' he replied. I later discovered he'd had a heart attack the day before.

Such understatement was also often the prelude to a ferocious pub argument about sheep, however, when discretion and reticence took a back seat to invective and insult.

'Now I'm going to tell you something that you may not just agree with,' said Chris, a big raw-boned man, with a habit of talking out of the side of his mouth, as if all his conversation was in confidence. Ten seconds later, having expressed his opinion about a particular tup (local dialect for a ram), he had brought the place into uproar, with farmers shouting, waving walking-sticks and banging on the table, red-faced with rage.

'Aren't you going to do anything?' enquired a middle-aged tourist couple, anxiously eyeing the distance to the door.

'What about?' I replied, sporting my newly-acquired upland nonchalance, 'It's only a mild disagreement.'

Amongst the warring factions arguing about sheep until the early hours, were a remarkable collection of characters. There was Bob Mick, perhaps the last man alive to have earned a living as a drover, buying up sheep from the fells and driving them to market as much as fifty miles away. Few farmers then took their own stock to market, and Mick and his partner would assemble a drove of several hundred wether (castrated male) lambs, buying them a few at a time for around eight shillings each, from the farms straddling the hills and selling them at market for a profit of as little as threepence a head.

His face was an astonishing assemblage of pouches and folds of skin, and his stories of old times were spellbinding, though many gems were lost somewhere between his susurrating speech, the local dialect and the tobacco juice sloshing about in his cheeks. Although we did possess toilets, Mick preferred the great outdoors and was often to be found, even on Bank Holidays, unselfconsciously relieving himself against the outside wall of the porch, as the throngs of holidaymakers milled around him.

Maud too was unique, a lady as old as the century, who lived in a small cottage in a nearby village with her eccentric son and nine cats. Well-bred and well-educated, Maud could nonetheless curse like a trooper and knew every dingy taproom from the Scottish border to the South of England. Every morning she would be carried to the pub in the back of the Post Office van – strictly against regulations, but the postmen were friendly sorts and head office was a long way away – lying on a pile of mail sacks, as the van bounced and bucketed up and down the farm tracks. While the postman had a cup of tea, Maud would order up a succession of 'Large whisky and soda, for the love of God', while chain-smoking untipped cigarettes.

Having tucked away five or six double whiskies in fifteen minutes, she would depart for home with a couple of bottles of Guinness and more cigarettes and whisky, to see her through until the next day. Her face was as wrinkled as an old hiking boot, and her liver must have been the size and appearance of a pickled walnut, but her mind was razor sharp and she kept us in fits of laughter with her invariably scurrilous tales of past misdeeds.

Jack lived at an old station on the disused Stainmore railway line, with spectacular views out over Eden. He was a gnarled, wizened, permanently unshaven, old man, who looked like a Steptoe without a son. He drove a battered pick-up truck and made a precarious living buying and selling things that even a scrap dealer like Neville would have looked at twice.

He produced scarcely edible butter and sour cream made from the milk from his Jersey cow. He sold logs cut from decrepit railway sleepers, so thick with creosote that the stench of them burning could be smelt miles away, and in his enthusiasm for a cheap purchase he often bought things that even he couldn't sell. I called round one day and spent half an hour helping him to unload a wooden hen house, bought at auction, that was so rotten that it collapsed as we were lifting it down from the wagon. 'Needs a bit of work' was Jack's only comment as we carried the sodden pieces of wood over to a corner of the yard and added them to an already mouldering heap of nameless, unidentifiable items.

Jack's only garb was a boiler suit. He possessed three of them, and selected them according to the business of the day. Two seemed to my untrained eye to be almost equally filthy, but Jack clearly held one in higher esteem, for he would never wear it while tackling really dirty jobs. His third boiler suit was immaculate, a Sunday-best outfit. When he appeared in that, I knew that the day was a rest day and that he was off somewhere important, perhaps to attend a wedding or see his bank manager.

Then there was Michael, who would argue as rancorously as the rest, brandishing his walking-stick at his foes like the greatest swordsman in all France, but who would haul himself upright at the end of the evening, leaning heavily on his stick, and sing the local anthems like an angel, reducing even the most truculent drunk to respectful silence. Jimmy, as round, pink, scrubbed and shining as a new-born baby, would tell the most wildly implausible tales, but was such good company that nobody minded in the least whether they were true or not; but above all there was Dick, who epitomized all the virtues of the uplander, and had none of the faults.

His eyes were hazel and hawk-sharp, his face weather-beaten and his hair iron grey, with a cap so permanently perched on it that it seemed to be stitched there. He had a chest like a barrel and a neck you could have bent iron bars around and, even at sixty years old, his relentless stride up the fells had me gasping for breath as I tried to keep up. His smile was as warming as the glow of a fire on a winter's day and his sense of humour as subtle as peat smoke in the wind. I never heard him speak a harsh word to or about anyone, and I heard nothing but admiration, liking and respect for him. The cliché 'one of nature's gentlemen' is, for once, wholly apt.

Many uplanders shun strangers, disinterested in the world outside their 'heaf', but Dick had a healthy curiosity about people and would join strangers in conversation, chuckling with delight at the ways of the world beyond his patch of ground. Despite this, he had made only one journey out of the area in his life, travelling to London for the Smithfield show. He got off the train at Kings Cross, stood aghast in the middle of the hordes of scurrying travellers and commuters, saw the traffic clogging the road outside, heard the noise, saw the dirt, smelt the air and caught the next train back to the North, without ever leaving the station.

Amongst this throng of remarkable characters, was Ben Alderson, whose tall, spare, long-striding figure, fair hair and eyes the pale, almost translucent blue of a clear winter sky, signalled his linear descent from the Norse who settled the uplands a thousand years ago. The names of virtually every landscape feature – fell, beck, rigg, hag, scar, tarn, dale – derive from the Norse, as does the upland dialect, to such an extent that many words – 'gimmer' for female is one – remain the same in both modern Norwegian and local speech. Scandinavians can often make more sense of the dialect than British visitors, to whose ears it can sound as harsh and incomprehensible as the cawing of the rooks in the trees.

The Aldersons' home territory is in Swaledale, where there are so many that, in order to distinguish one from another, they are either known by a name like Pat Jack or Dick Ned, combining their own and their father's Christian names, or by linking their name with the name of their farm, like 'Dick at Greenses' or 'Bill at Thorns', or by a nickname like 'Gurt Bill up t'steps'. That nickname identified Big Bill Anderson, who lived in a house up a flight of steps, a rarity amongst the farms of the dale. When he grew old and moved to a bungalow in Gunnerside, he was instantly re-christened 'Bungalow Bill' instead.

Since Ben farms over the tops in Eden, where Aldersons are less thick on the ground, he is able to survive with a single Christian name. Ben is as shrewd and observant as any hill farmer, and he weighs his utterances carefully, often pausing in mid-sentence for a few seconds to re-examine his thought before committing it to words, but he is also refreshingly free of the narrow, blinkered world view that can afflict people in small agricultural communities. Perhaps the rolling fells and broad acres of the land he farms encourage wide perspectives and far horizons; perhaps the Eden, ever-enduring but ever-changing, reminds him that even the thousand years that his ancestors have farmed by its banks, are less than the cry of a curlew in the life of the river.

# ·W·INTER·

THE soft, white, midwinter light touches the moor tops and the slopes, but barely penetrates the dark, frozen gullies, hidden from the sun throughout the winter months. The constant drip of water from the sodden peat has been stilled by the cold. Grey rock, like bone, juts from the frozen fell. The first red warning of sunset streaks the sky and frost settles even deeper into the ice-bound, grit-hard ground. Nothing moves in a brittle, skeletal landscape.

By dawn wind-driven cloud scouring over the frost-bitten land in the night has encased every rock, plant stem, grass blade and wire strand in a thin sheath of ice. The wind stills at dawn to a whisper, gently soughing over the fell, stirring the ice-coated rushes in a clinking and tinkling that drifts down the breeze. A grouse raises its head grumpily from a patch of heather on the skyline, its call echoing around the frozen peat hags.

# 2
# BLACK FELL
# MOSS

Lady Anne's Pillar

Eden journey did not arise for five years, but when at last I was
free to travel through Eden, the timing seemed irresistible.
Along the length of the river, the old communities were in their
death throes, as the ripples from the Southern property boom
reached even into this far corner of the land. I could make the
journey I had promised myself, and I could be there at the last
rites of old Eden – paradise lost to an uncertain future.

There was by now a further compelling reason for me to
make the journey. Sue and I had left the inn after managing it
for a year, vowing to return as owners. Five years later, having
completed the shady dealings with Neville, we returned in
triumph to that isolated Pennine hilltop; but a venture begun
on a wave of optimism foundered within two years. I left the
pub a wealthier man, certainly, but having suffered a double
personal loss.

With my close family recently dead and my marriage
broken, I fled Britain to spend six months travelling around the
world, but then returned to buy a house within ten miles of the
pub, perhaps seeing in the enduring mass of the fells and the
stability of village life a counter-weight to the turbulence of my
personal life. Like an adopted family, the small community in
which I lived nurtured me back to health and confidence.
Then, like an ingrate son, I began to chafe at the restrictions of
village life, and moved on.

The journey through Eden offered the welcome chance
to renew acquaintance with my adopted family and with my
erstwhile customers and friends from the days at the pub in the
hills. My initial destination was Ben's farm up on the fells

surrounding the source of the Eden. The farm would provide me with Base Camp One for my expedition into Eden and a place of refuge if the winter weather turned against me. I had only to settle the matter of my equipment and supplies and I could begin my voyage of discovery.

I consulted the oracle, William Boot, the hero of Evelyn Waugh's *Scoop*, probably the most comprehensively equipped journalist ever to set forth on an assignment. In addition to a set of cleft sticks, 'Boot of the Beast' took with him, 'a well-, perhaps rather over-, furnished tent, three months' rations, a collapsible canoe, a jointed flagstaff and Union Jack, a hand-pump and sterilizing plant, an astrolabe, six suits of tropical linen and a sou'-wester, a camp operating table and set of surgical instruments, a portable humidor, guaranteed to preserve cigars in condition in the Red Sea, a Christmas hamper complete with Santa Claus costume and a tripod mistletoe stand, and a cane for whacking snakes . . . At the last moment he added a coil of rope and a sheet of tin.'

Although Boot's baggage seemed to encompass most possibilities, I felt that it was slightly better suited to travel in North Africa than Northern England, and I compiled instead a list of the things a true hikesman – a Hiking Boot – would require to face the Pennines with confidence. A stout pair of boots, tins of dubbin, a dozen pairs of thick wool socks, waterproof gaiters like overgrown spats, bristling with hooks and eyes, thick wool knee breeches, thermal underwear, wool shirts and coarse, hairy pullovers, bilious yellow waterproof jacket and leggings, embarrassing woolly hat with bobble, gloves, compass, clear plastic container to be hung round the neck on a string, keeping the Ordnance Survey map dry, visible and dangling always within reach, rucksack, tent, sleeping bag, inflatable mattress, foil blankets, windproof matches, iron rations, primus stove, billy cans, water bottle, chocolate bars, tea bags, water sterilizing tablets, needle and thread, travel Scrabble, army-style survival guide explaining how to extract protein from crushed cockroaches, whistle, torch, first aid kit, short wave radio, distress flares, Verey pistol, length of rope, Swiss army penknife, binoculars, field guides to the mammals, birds, fish, reptiles, invertebrates, trees, plants, ferns, grasses, flowers, fungi, rocks, minerals and soils of Northern England, dictionary of Cumbrian dialect, Bible and complete works of Shakespeare.

In my time at the fell-top inn, I had seen many similarly equipped hikers on the Pennine Way and derived much simple pleasure from the sight of them toiling up the fell-sides, like snails with leaden shells. On a cloudless summer day, I went to the assistance of one Pennine wayfarer, who was unable to walk another step. Scarcely able to pick up his rucksack for him, I discovered that among the customary tent poles, socks and pullovers were a dozen large tins of baked beans, stew and vegetables. He was in no danger of starvation, just death from exhaustion.

A nearby patch of glutinous ground proved a particularly valuable source of entertainment. One man who slipped and fell while traversing it was so weighed down by his pack that he was unable to raise himself unassisted and lay there on his back, waving his arms and legs in the air like a demented tortoise, until a rescue party, weak with laughter, came to his aid.

Another unfortunate leaned too far forward and found the weight of his pack propelling him relentlessly forward, till he was face-down in the bog. He emerged looking and sounding like the Creature from the Black Lagoon, a peat-smothered hulk, emitting banshee wails of disgust.

If I were to avoid a similarly hideous fate, it was clear that either I would have to use bearers to carry my equipment or else restrict myself to the bare necessities. The thought of a Sir Gandalf Twickenham District Lines-style expedition had enormous appeal: twelve major sponsors, a thousand tons of supplies borne by a massive motorized convoy and a send-off from a member of the royal family, watched by a battery of the international press, as a moist-eyed, society beauty wrang her exquisitely manicured hands in distress at my departure. It was an appealing image, but it seemed a trifle implausible for a sixty-mile journey through well-charted English territory and I set it aside, not without some regret.

I toyed with the idea of a 'Five Discover the Eden Valley' expedition instead. Plenty of scrumptious picnics with hard-boiled eggs, fruit cake and lots of ginger pop, and an Adventure in which I and my companions, including George (short for Georgina) who always had wanted to be a boy, and Christopher (long for Christine) who always had not, would discover secret caves and smugglers, while Timmy the dog chased sheep all over the fells, before being shot by an irate farmer. This, too, failed the plausibility test and I decided reluctantly that Eden was a journey that I had to make alone. I tossed a pair of wellingtons, a map and a Mars bar into the car and set off for the hills on a grey December day.

Ben Alderson's sheep graze the high and lonely moors where the headwaters of the Eden ooze and trickle from the saturated peat of Black Fell Moss, a spit of land sloping down from the summit of Hugh Seat, drained by becks flowing down Little Grain and Red Gill to Hell Gill – 'the stygian rivulet flowing through a horrid silent wilderness', in the jaundiced view of Camden's sixteenth-century *Britannica*. I had called on Ben for a cup of tea to ward off the December chill, before climbing up to the source of the Eden, secure in the promise of a hot dinner and a bed for the night on my return. We chatted a few minutes, then he watched me set off up the hill with the amused tolerance displayed by farmers towards those who walk for pleasure rather than need.

In this wind-swept, rain-soaked land, any one of a myriad dark, still pools or trickling streams, flowing from the black sponge of the Moss, could pass for the source of the Eden. I chose a curtain of drips of water falling constantly from a small overhang of peat, a few yards from a rough stone pillar, and watched the water trickling slowly away towards Hell Gill.

The surface of the pillar is incised with the initials of Anne, Countess of Pembroke, who had it erected in 1664 to mark the source of the Eden. This delight of local historians and travellers through Eden remains undiscovered by Ben Alderson. Like all hill farmers, he knows his patch of a few square miles of land more intimately and thoroughly than a city dweller could even imagine, but since the pillar can neither feed nor shelter his sheep, its inscriptions and its origins hold no great attraction for him.

'There are some stones up on the top, with lettering on them, aren't there?' said Ben, when I asked him about the pillar, on my return from the hills, late in the afternoon. 'I've been by them many a time, but I've never had time to stop and look.'

From high on the Moss, only a couple of miles of the course of Hell Gill Beck can be seen, before it dips from sight behind the shoulder of one of the relentless tide of dun-coloured hills, rolling away like a vast ocean swell. Before I followed the beck down from the moor I wanted to see Eden once more as I remembered it from five years before, and as countless cross-Pennine travellers down the centuries, wearied by the endless expanses of moor, moss and fell, had seen it: a green and beautiful oasis appearing suddenly before them in a brown, waterlogged desert.

I crossed the top of the Moss, a strange, almost lunar landscape, punctuated by hags and hummocks of peat capped with heather. Surrounding them is the grey, gritstone bedrock, stripped bare by the force of erosion, leaving only sterile, rain-washed ground. If split, the rock is a surprising coral pink, but a few weeks of wind and weather leach the colour from it, leaving it as grey as the clouds streaming over the fells.

Lower on the slopes, spiders' webs, jewelled with moisture from the clouds, glowed among the mat grass in the watery sunlight. A grouse clattered out from beneath my feet, whirring away downwind as I blundered from wiry tussocks of heather into mosses and bogs, the ground quaking gently, as if there was nothing solid in these water-filled hills. At each step, the peat gave up its hold on my boots with a soft, reproachful sound.

Down a short slope of sheep-cropped turf, past the ruins

of a sheepfold, the Eden Valley suddenly opens up. Directly across is the knife-edge of The Nab on Wild Boar Fell, where Hell Gill's twin, Ais Gill, begins its plunge down to feed the Eden. A kestrel hung in the air, tossed on the wind like a handful of rags. I stood high on the edge, above the precipitous screes of Hangingstone Scar, leaning against the wind, watching the river as it curved away to the north.

Below the screes, grass-covered mounds of boulder clay and rock rubble stud the plateau, abandoned by the Ice Age glacier which ground its way through Mallerstang, as this part of the valley is known. The moor presses down hard on the valley sides, but on either bank of the river are a patchwork of pastures and meadows, filling the valley floor and maintaining a precarious hold on the lower slopes, a ribbon of fertility in a barren land.

The next day, the omens for my intended departure down the Eden are not good. Cloud like pewter begins to mass over the fells. A wary stillness falls, broken only by the gabble of a grouse and the anxious bleat of a sheep. As the light fades, the snow starts. The first few flakes drift by in the wind, thin white flecks, dry on the skin, lodging for a second in a skein of grass, then drifting down to the frozen peat.

At first only a grey dust seems to settle, but as the wind grows, the driven flecks coat and whiten the moor. Dusk is held back as light reflects from the snow, but the land now appears fluid, shifting and changing as the snow flurries blur and soften familiar landmarks.

I stand scanning the snow clouds anxiously, as Ben takes a last look over his sheep, clustered around the hay he has scattered, then I follow him as he strides down the hill to his three-wheeler, one of many recent changes in a shepherd's life on these fells. 'We got rid of our last horse a year ago. We've always used them for shepherding, but we use iron horses, three-wheelers and the like, now.' The engine kicks into life and we wheel away from the fell, his dogs chasing behind, crossing and re-crossing the tyre tracks down towards Hell Gill.

The engine note is carried away on the wind, as the snow continues to fall.

In less than an hour the moor is smothered in white, broken only by the thin, dark striations of rush stalks and a few black outcrops of rock. Even these features fade as the wind continues to strengthen, the snow erasing all recognition in a whirling, blurring, blinding white-out.

Even a farmer's lifetime knowledge of his land would now be of little use, for no landmark nor familiar perspective remains and even the wind seems to swing from quarter to quarter. In a white-out a man may be hopelessly lost within yards of his house, not knowing which way to turn, hoping only for an easing of the storm or a momentary dulling of the wind to give him a familiar glimpse or sound to guide him home.

I was once lost for a few frightening minutes up at the inn, uncertain whether I had already crossed the snow-covered road I was seeking and scarcely able to see or hear for the snow and the wind. Then I was lucky, for a momentary drop in the wind allowed me to hear the dull thud of the diesel engine of the generator. I had already passed the pub without realizing it, and was heading on towards the open fell. I wondered whether Ben had ever been similarly confused in a storm. If so, he was not admitting it.

'I've never been lost in a white-out. I've been on the moor often enough when it's been bad, but you still tend to find where you're at. You don't set off on those particular days when it's very bad, there is always a break when it eases off a bit, so we try to be out when the weather is kind of decent. If it comes on bad, I always preach to my own lads to be aiming for home regardless. You don't want to be stuck fast away out over those tops or you might never be seen again.'

At the farm far below, Ben feeds his dogs, then we battle the wind across the yard and kick the snow from our boots against his doorstep. The fells are hidden from sight by the snow clouds as night falls. High on the tops, his sheep must take their chances on the open fell, driven themselves, like the snow, before the wind. When the storm subsides, perhaps tomorrow, perhaps not for several days, we must again set out for the moor to find them.

On the following day, the storm blows almost without interruption. We set off in one lull, but turn for home without reaching the moor when the wind regains strength and begins to drive the snow into fresh drifts. By the next morning, however, the storm has blown itself out, leaving the snow piled in huge drifts wherever a wall, a bluff or a drop in the ground has slackened the wind, causing part of its burden of snow to fall. Other exposed areas have been scoured clear by the wind; dark, bare patches, almost shocking in their contrast to the aching expanses of white.

We are up on the fell early. A few groups of sheep are visible, standing immobile, fleece-deep in snow, but many more are lost, buried in gills, behind walls and in a host of other places. They all must be located and dug out, but first we start the long and arduous process of leading a group of sheep down to the foddering ground, a patch of moor swept clear of snow by the wind. In deep snow the sheep either cannot or will not move unaided and we must first make a path, trampling a way through the snow for a few yards, then dragging one reluctant sheep along it. 'If the snow's that deep, usually you can't shift them until you have wandered a track through a big deep drift to set them off; but with sheep, if one goes, the rest will follow, they all go.'

Neither frost nor thaw have yet worked upon the snow, which is as soft and powdery as talc. A drift will bear no weight at all, each footfall sinks deep and there is no purchase to aid the next step. I drop into a snow-filled gully and flounder helplessly for a minute, struggling to compress the snow enough to clamber out. Ben's keener eye had detected a difference in the snow over the gully and he skirted it, pausing to watch my struggles with amusement.

Once the visible sheep have been moved and foddered, we begin the search for the buried ewes. Struggling up the snow along a gill side, Ben's dog 'sets' a buried sheep, her nostrils picking up the faint scent through the drift. She begins scrabbling down through the snow, but Ben calls her off and five minutes' digging with a shovel breaks through to two bedraggled ewes, little the worse for their 48 hours beneath the snow.

I asked Ben about this gift some dogs have for finding sheep under the snow.

'Not many have it. We've been gare fortunate that way, we always seem to have had one. In my time, I've just had three out of near on a hundred dogs at one time and another with the knack.'

'How long would the sheep have lasted, if we hadn't found them?'

'If a sheep is buried under a drift, it could last a long time, unless it's thawed pretty fast and a big weight of snow has come down on it. It depends on the time of year; if it's January or February, when they're not too heavy with lamb, they could last up to a fortnight, but you try to find them within a week, if you know where to look, that's the point, like. They'll often get in gills, and follow them away down out of the wind and often enough, you'll find them at the back of walls, buried five or six foot deep. It's pretty good for a dog to sniff them out of those sort of places, you know, but you can imagine over a wide area, there are a lot of places where you can bury sheep; there are a lot of places where you can bury a man, like.'

The young 'hoggs', the previous spring's lambs, are wintered down country on the softer lands of the valley floor, but for the mature sheep of the breeding flock, the moors around the head of the Eden, straddling the border between Yorkshire and Cumbria, are the only home they know. 'We keep them up there all winter, we'll never have had them off the moors in the thirty years I've farmed here.'

They are 'heafed' to the moors, in the local phrase, only straying from them when driven against their will. So strong is the pull of the heaf that when a farm changes hands, the sheep are always sold with it as part of the deal. They remain up on the tops in all but the wildest weather, surviving on a diet that would starve their fat lowland cousins. Like their ancestors described by William Marshall in 1808, they are 'peculiarly adapted to the extreme bleakness of the climature and the extreme coarseness of the herbage. They live upon the open heaths the year round. Their food, heath, rushes and a few of the coarsest grasses; a pasture on which, perhaps, any other breed of sheep would starve.'

The farmers were once as strongly heafed to the land as their stock, but, while the older men will rarely have been out of sight of their land from one year to the next, some sons now take package holidays in Majorca. Poor communications and the slow spread of electrification held back the pace of change in the uplands for many years, but television culture is eroding local dialect and tradition now as relentlessly as the Eden cuts away at the soil. The song got it wrong; the real question is: 'How are you going to keep them down on the farm, now that they've seen TV?'

The daily routine of gathering in the sheep to the sheltered area, where they are foddered with hay, ensures that if a storm breaks, the task of feeding and finding them after the storm has passed will be less difficult . . . providing that the wind has not also scattered them all over the fells that separate Eden from the Yorkshire Dales.

A 'lazy' east wind, one that can't be bothered to go round you and cuts straight through you instead, can drive a flock of sheep before it literally for miles. They huddle before it like penguins in the Antarctic, those on the windward side continually peeling off and running round to the leeward side, leaving the next rank exposed to the biting cold.

The sheep will try to find what protection they can, an old sheepfold, the lee of a wall or a patch of ground out of the line of the wind, but on these exposed tops there are few places to hide. 'It can be bad when the wind settles into the east, though up Hell Gill you've a job to find shelter anywhere, if it's that sort of weather. We try to feed them where there is some shelter, but they'll tend to clutter up in a big heap when it's like that and keep circling around the flock away from the wind. It plays a big part if there's a blizzard blowing. If you're stuck out there and you can get at the back of a wall it's not so bad, but if you can't. . .'

I needed no reminding of the ferocity of the east wind, for our first year at the inn had included the cruel winter of 1979, one of the hardest in the North since the war, with an east wind blowing for weeks on end. The friendly pub owners took part of the central heating boiler away at the end of September – 'to get it repaired,' they said – but they didn't bring it back until the next spring. We had no central heating and very quickly no water either, because every drop in the place froze. The main generator broke down too, not surprisingly, because they would never pay to have it serviced, so we had no light or power unless we ran the stand-by generator.

Outside the wind was icing everything, it was like being on a trawler in the Arctic, with every metal surface buried under a thick coating of ice. If I put the small generator outside, the air inlet would be covered in ice in ten minutes and the engine would cut out, but if I brought it inside, the whole building would fill with diesel fumes. The final straw came when I was trying to move it from outside. The wheels were iced to the ground and I was heaving away trying to shift it. In the end the only things that weren't frozen to the ground were my feet. I slipped and broke my two front teeth in half on the casing of the generator.

After that we made do with candles, and when they ran out, we went to bed when the sun went down or just sat in the firelight. I couldn't get out to see a dentist for ten days, and I was reduced to drinking bottles of Guinness through a straw and screaming every time any cold air touched my teeth. When the weather finally did ease down, I had to walk five miles through the snow to reach a bit of road that had been cleared; they were digging the snow out with JCBs. At the edge of the moor I was walking level with the tops of the walls, because the road was completely buried under the drifts. While my broken teeth ensured that I would forever remember the winter of 'seventy-nine as the worst one of my lifetime, Ben favoured an earlier one.

'That was bad enough, like, but I think 'sixty-three was worse. It started snowing about Boxing Day and it seemed to snow every day till about the middle of March. It froze every night, till it was as solid as concrete. It's desperate weather when it's like that day in and day out. It's the wind that does the havoc. There'll be a 'Helm wind' down the bottom of the valley and it fills the road up constantly when that Helm wind's blowing. That was the first year that mains electricity came into Mallerstang, 'sixty-three. Before that, it was all oil lamps and a few of the old Lister generators. Hard to credit now, isn't it?'

What Ben and all hill farmers dread most is a storm that breaks without real warning, giving them no time to gather their sheep and lead them to safer, more sheltered ground. 'In 1980 there was a tremendous storm at lambing time that no one would ever expect. It blew up drastic out of the blue, because the day before had been a mild day. I'd been out on the fells, gathering in sheep ready for lambing. It was a lovely, red hot day.

'At night it was as quiet as it is now, but the next morning, when we got up, it was snowing. It had whitened all over, but that was nothing unusual for that time of year. You could often get a snow in the night, but it would usually have gone by dinner time. This time it never did, it just kept snowing and snowing and by night it had got quite a lot on. Then it got to blowing and there was a tremendous weight of snow, we had forever of stuff – stock – buried under the snow.

'We were around the middle of lambing time. We lost about fifty lambs that would be born that day; as they were born they were buried, they never got a chance to get up. I know we had an awful lot, it kept us going doing nowt else but digging out sheep for days. At the end of it we'd lost very few yows – adult sheep as you might say – we lost a few hoggs that we'd not turned out on the moor so long, but on the whole we came off well with the situation as it was. With lambs you can't expect nowt else, they would only be a week old or less and it just buried them wherever they were, there was that much snow in a short time, and drifted too.'

'Have you ever been really hit badly by losses in snow?'

'I never have, it would be a rare thing today, but in 1947 there would be chaps up this valley just about wiped out by the storms. One local man moved on to a hill farm at the start of February, just before the snow began. He took over 500 ewes and finished up, three months later, with 170 ewes and 12 lambs.'

'So what made the difference then, was it just the ferocity of the weather?'

'Well, sheep wouldn't be fed the same as they are today, they would never really have had enough feed about and hay would be bad to get hold of. Well, I suppose they soon starve to death, does stuff, if they don't get plenty to eat in what we call hungry weather, when the severe east winds are on. They're not getting much anywhere else if it's that bad and the ground's frozen up, they're just going to get what you give them.

'Now we give sheep the likes of sugar beet, which keeps them up, but in 1947 they would never get any other feed than hay. Well it would be too long a storm, wouldn't it, and they wouldn't have enough to eat. I would say that would be the top and bottom of it. They will only stand so much, will stuff, before they'll crack up.'

We turned back down the moor at the top of the Moss, above Red Gill, where a new wire fence runs along the ridge. Boundaries were once defined by natural landmarks and by watersheds – 'as Heaven water deals', as the old documents say – but these ancient boundaries across the moors are now reinforced by miles of wire fencing, stretching into the distance. The wires carry the signals of a profound change in the pattern of upland life.

A boom in income from grouse shooting has persuaded some of the larger landowners to buy up the 'stints', the grazing rights on the moors, and remove the sheep. The land is fenced to prevent stock straying from the adjoining moors, although it has the added benefit from the landowners' point of view, of restricting access for hikers and other would-be intruders on their selfish pleasures. Farms are bought as they come up for sale or tenants are persuaded or 'sweetened' to move. The farms obtained are split up, the City of London would perhaps call it 'asset-stripped', with the farmhouse sold as a private house, the pasture and meadow land rented to one of the handful of remaining farmers, though 'ranchers' might now be a more appropriate term, and the grazing rights on the moor retained by the landowner, but not used.

This practice has already blighted Swaledale, just to the East, applying the *coup de grâce* to farming communities that had survived, little altered for a thousand years. The uplands above Eden will do well to avoid the same fate. The belief is that fewer sheep will mean more grouse, but the case is far from proven, or universally accepted. Ben Alderson's view is shared by most local people, by no means all of them farmers with axes to grind. 'Well I wouldn't think you'll get more grouse if you take the sheep off, there'll be a balance, won't there, always will have been. The heather will tend to get too rough without the sheep, because the grouse won't keep it down, there has to be something that's going to eat it.'

'But haven't you farmers been overstocking?' I asked. 'If you can get a subsidy on every sheep you have, surely that encourages you to keep a few extra?'

'No, I wouldn't say so. Most farmers here tend to keep what they can handle. They are all to winter, you needn't have them if there are more than you can winter. I wouldn't think there would be many more sheep than ever there was.'

At the moor edge, we stopped by the evidence of an earlier land-grab by the large landowners, one of the ubiquitous Pennine drystone walls. Most date from the eighteenth and early nineteenth centuries, when an avalanche of Enclosure Acts passed through Parliament. The House of Commons proved no friend to the holders of commons rights, for those who could not afford to pay their share of the cost of enclosure forfeited them. By a cruel irony, men forced off their land into dependency on others, often found the only available work was in building the walls enclosing the land that had once been their own.

The House of Lords predictably proved to be no better friend to the drovers, overturning their historic rights of 'stance and passage' across the moors and commons in a test case in the 1840s. The comments in the *London Daily News* at the time would need little alteration to fit the activities of the present large landowners: 'Rights of road, especially footpaths and driftways over enclosed land have been almost annihilated in England, and the Highland proprietors of Scotland seem to be rapidly effecting the same thing . . . There is too much reason to fear that the encroaching proprietor with an ultimate right of appeal to a tribunal of his own class will be more than a match for the public . . . This right of stance, which has existed for centuries, is not displaced to make way for cultivation or improvement of any kind, but to foster the barbarous and puerile passion for artificial wild sports, and the feudal spirit of the House of Lords assists the purblind owners of Highland Estates to push their proprietary right to this mischievous extreme.'

Already exhausted by my struggles through the snow, I took a slightly shame-faced leave of Ben at the moor edge, returning to the warmth of the farmhouse for a bath and a rest, leaving him to carry on with his work until dark. I watched him striding back up through the snow to his sheep, before I turned downhill, leaden-footed towards the road. When I reached the farm, I looked up again towards the fells and saw him still moving across the snow, a speck as black as a crow in a wilderness of white.

# 3
# HELL GILL
# AND
# MALLERSTANG

Hell Gill

THE STORM HAD BEEN AS BRIEF AS

it was ferocious. The wind swung away from the east, and warm south–westerlies started the melting snow on its journey down the Eden to the sea. Within a few days, the snow had already gone from the moor top, though it still coated the north sides of the gills and gullies, where it might cling stubbornly until May. I had trudged up from Ben's farm, far below, on a cool January morning, to start my journey through Eden, reaching the beck where it tumbles fast down a rocky, boulder-strewn course to the plateau. There it meanders more gently for a while, gathering its strength for the wild, breakneck plunge down through the gorge of Hell Gill.

I followed it downstream, crossing and re-crossing the beck in its narrow valley, cut off from distant views by the steep sides of the gill. Every few hundred yards another stream adds its weight, and, though the beck itself it still scarcely more than a mountain stream, its destructive power in spate is already obvious from the collapsed banks and landslips, the outside of each bend scarred by fresh erosion.

These treeless wastes may have a look of timelessness and permanence, but the young river emphasizes that nothing is constant. Hillsides are poised on the brink of slipping into the water below, and even the largest boulders will eventually be cracked and broken by the force of wind, rain and frost. A flood will carry them off, breaking them, grinding them, turning rock into gravel and silt that will one day be carried by the Eden to the sea.

I fought my way through a chest-high forest of rushes, startling a brace of wild duck, which flighted off, arcing up high over the shoulder of the hill ahead, where the valley walls open out and the beck disappears into the depths of the gorge from which it takes its name.

The rocks above the head of the gorge are deeply marked with the spoor of water erosion. When there has been little rain, the beck flows gently through the gorge, spilling from one pool of brown, peaty water to another. When in spate, it is filled with a roaring torrent of angry, foaming water, which backs up above the head of the chasm, flooding the surrounding land, unable to force its way fast enough through the narrow gap. The gorge is one hundred feet deep, yet the sides are close enough to jump across, were it not for the thought of that long drop if you fall short. I leaned over the old stone bridge across the gorge instead, the air dank, moist and rich in early summer with the damp smell of wild garlic.

The bridge forms part of a green road dating back at least to the Bronze Age. Generally called the High Way, it is also known as Lady Anne's Way, in honour of Lady Anne Clifford, the Countess of Pembroke commemorated on the stone pillar on the fell above, who used the road on her journeys between her castles in Yorkshire and Westmorland.

A trade route for thousands of years, this way through Mallerstang also provided the Scots with an invasion route during centuries of border raiding, a break in the Pennines opening the way to Skipton, Richmond and the Plain of York. The chain of crumbling castles at the head of Mallerstang and throughout Eden testifies to its former importance. Long after the raiding had ceased, it remained in use by Scots drovers, pack-horse trains, pedlars and travellers until well into the nineteenth century, even after the construction of a turnpike along the valley bottom.

Turnpikes were hated by drovers, pedlars, carriers, miners and farmers, who saw in them benefit only for the rich or even felt their own livelihood threatened. Toll bars were destroyed and 'pikemen', whose duty was to collect the tolls, were assaulted. A vengeful Parliament responded with punishments ranging from public whipping to transportation or 'death without clergy'.

Like all ancient tracks, the High Way follows a line along
the shoulder of the hills, using the well-drained plateaux,
particularly on the limestone, which gave far easier passage
than the thickly-forested swamps of the valley floor. North of
the bridge, it still provides a magnificent walk along the
limestone scarp. A low ridge masks the upper slopes for a time,
before the stunning sight of Hangingstone Scar and Mallerstang Edge appears high to the east, while the whole length of
Mallerstang – 'the marsh of the wild duck' – is laid out ahead.
The Eden disappears from sight at the far end, as if locked in a
blind valley with a river flowing to nowhere, hemmed in on all
sides by hills.

As it descends through rough pasture towards the river,
the track becomes progressively more uneven and muddy;
hard going in a modern four-wheel drive, close to impossible in
an old horse-drawn carriage. A remark by Ben Alderson came
back to me as I negotiated the mud and rocks of Lady Anne's
Way: 'You wouldn't credit someone flying through here in a
coach, it would be a roughish ride, because they wouldn't be
that well sprung, would they?'

In fact it was Lady Anne's attendants who suffered the
exquisite agony of the coach, for she preferred the unusual
arrangement of travel in a horse litter, slung between two
horses, which, though it would have swung about alarmingly at
times, prevented the kind of terminal kidney failure that a long
journey in a coach over such tracks would guarantee.

Whenever she or any of the nobility was travelling, a posse
of retainers was always in attendance and they would
frequently be required to manhandle the carriage through the
mud along the way. So awful were the roads before turnpiking
that some nobles actually travelled in carriages pulled by
bullocks, as horses were not strong enough to cope with the
mud on the worst routes. Travel was almost exclusively a
summer occupation; in winter many roads became completely
impassable.

The High Way cuts the modern road at Thrang, crossing
the river, no longer a beck, at Thrang Bridge. A dipper flew

ahead of me downriver, pausing every few hundred yards, its white bib catching the light as it bobbed and curtseyed on a rock in mid-stream, before it flew off again at my approach. I passed a group of farm buildings, a patchwork of multicoloured sheets of rusting corrugated metal, not entirely in the local vernacular tradition, and followed the bank through a delightful wood, the river forming a green, dark tunnel beneath the canopy of the trees, to the hamlet of Shoregill.

Once slipping into apparently terminal decline, Shoregill is now alive again, its old stone houses all occupied by purposeful newcomers, busily restoring and renovating. The 'horrid' and 'frightful' landscape described by sixteenth- and seventeenth-century travellers has become infinitely desirable to twentieth-century eyes.

While 'offcomers' are not always welcomed in rural areas, their presence in Mallerstang has been perhaps less traumatic than most. The explosion of property values came later here than the rest of the country, and the strangers bought mainly houses and barns that had long stood derelict. 'There is a big percentage of outsiders here now,' said a farmer I met near Shoregill, 'but they've done good in one respect, they've done up houses that would otherwise have gone to the wall. There's one just over there that nobody had been living in for thirty years.'

He settled his forearms along the top of a gate, preparing for a lengthy chat, a man to whom a rush was only a thing that grew in his pasture. He had a cigarette dangling from the corner of his mouth, carrying a precarious column of ash. He neither inhaled nor removed it from his mouth, content to allow the smoke to drift up into his eye without apparent discomfort. He was dressed in his working clothes, a cap settled on his head like a cowpat on a patch of grass and trousers which looked to have been acquired second-hand from a man two sizes bigger than him. They were held in place by an enormous pair of braces, reinforced by a stout leather belt. His shirt was the old-fashioned, striped, flannel variety, the separate collar long detached and probably lost altogether.

In contrast to the trousers, his short-sleeved, v-necked pullover was too small for him and holed below the waterline, riding up over his midriff to expose an ample waistline and an errant thong poking out from his braces. The jacket was functional rather than decorative, with enough encrustations to keep a forensic scientist busy for weeks. A piece of baler twine around his middle compensated for the missing buttons, and stuffing spilled out of the shoulder seams; it would have been no great surprise to find sparrows nesting there.

He talked a good deal of old days and hard times, but when I steered him back to the subject of newcomers, to my surprise, he showed no resentment of them. 'Most of the outsiders seem to fit in with the community, well enough. There are some people who maybe never fit in anywhere, but most of them seem to be very clannable people.'

'What about the visitors, though, the walkers and the tourists, how do you feel about them?'

'There's a tremendous lot of walkers, it's trebled these last few years. They can be a damned nuisance, they leave gates open, knock part of a wall down, with going over and this sort of thing, but there's a percentage of them very good, just a few who couldn't care less. It's not so bad if they stick to footpaths, but some tend to wander aimlessly anywhere.'

I pointed out that I had just walked down from the head of the dale, finding virtually none of the footpaths marked and almost all the stiles walled up, blocked or fenced off. It seemed less than just to blame the visitors for not knowing where the footpaths were supposed to be, when often it was the farmers themselves that were forcing them to climb over the walls.

'I would say it's better if the footpaths are clearly marked, it puts things out of dispute,' he said, steering a careful course round the topic of obstructed paths and blocked-up stiles. 'You never mind where anyone's going, if they close gates and don't do any damage. Dogs and that I don't like. These people coming with half a dozen dogs and they won't just keep them on leads. Well, they will if they see you, but turn your back and they're gone again, they're the worst type.'

'Would you ever shoot a visitor's dog?'

'I'd shoot a dog if it was chasing sheep, because you can't do with that. We keep our dogs under strict control, when we're not working them, they're tied up, we never give them chance, because there's some of them that would, what we call keen dogs that want a master. They are things that can do a lot of lumber, are dogs. These people that walk about with them tend to think you're shouting over nowt, they say "Oh, it's under control", but they don't realize what frightening sheep can do. They can rush off and maybe end up in the Eden somewhere, without the dog maybe even going after it, because it just alarms them. That's what we're up against though, because they're coming out more, these people, than ever before.'

I asked if he thought that visitors actually realized they were on private land, since the name 'National Park' might make them think of public parks which are purely for recreation.

'I sometimes reckon that they think they're in no-man's-land and it doesn't belong to anyone, the way they set off. They'll ramp about all over the place. I suppose some of them think that nobody lives here or no one owns it. The worst lot are those enthusiasts when they're running a steam train on the Settle–Carlisle. Good Lord above, there can be thousands of them and they just seem to go wild. They're over walls, knocking them down and they rush about as if there wasn't another minute for anything. If it was anybody on the road they would go over the top of you for two pins when they get set sail, because they go with some steam, like.'

'So do you get sick of the tourists?'

'No, I get sick of the ones that think the whole place grinds to a halt as soon as they go home. "What do you find to do in winter?" some of them ask, as if we hibernate when the visitors aren't here. So I tell them: "We sit around the fire and talk about all the daft buggers that come here in summer" – and as a rule that shuts them up.'

I left him shaking with laughter, still draped comfortably

over the gate, and I walked away from the born-again hamlet of Shoregill towards the river. One irony of this resurrection of the small communities is that, while the offcomers are enthusiastically buying and restoring the traditional Eden farmhouses, cottages and barns, the aspirations of the traditional Eden inhabitants are firmly directed towards modern, pebble-dashed bungalows. Bungalow bliss is now part of almost every village along the Eden.

While outsiders eulogize traditional stone farmhouses, oak beams and open fires, Eden natives see only damp walls, whistling draughts, awkward corners to be dusted and buckets of coal to be carried in and ashes carried out. We grow up in squeaky-clean modern houses, all straight lines and sharp angles and yearn for curving walls, lumpy ceilings, uneven floors and plumbing that goes bump in the night. We call it character; natives of Eden would probably call it a pain in the backside.

Alongside the ranks of new bungalows, another, increasingly prevalent feature of the Eden landscape is the mound of 'big bales' – large, black plastic bags in which grass, cut and 'siloed' as winter feed, is stored. It occupies a half-way point between hay and silage and has become very common in recent years, its advent spurred by a series of wet summers that has made haytime difficult or even impossible.

Though the hill farmers will always need some baled hay, the black-bagged stuff is much easier to get and is certain to replace most of the hay crop. I found the mounds of giant black plastic bags by almost every farm a depressing sight, both in themselves and as the harbinger of the final disappearance of the drystone field barns.

At one time virtually every hay meadow contained a stone barn. The hay would be pitchforked up into the hay mew in summer, and in winter it was dropped through a hole in the floor to feed a few cattle wintered in the stalls below. As mechanization and the use of big, steel-framed sheds closer to the farm has increased, however, the need for so many barns has correspondingly lessened. In most areas they will be gone

54

in fifty years, converted to houses or demolished, only surviving where regional sentiment or, more likely, the cash of National Parks persuades farmers to retain them.

Across the river is Outhgill, a village cluster of farms and buildings, stained by the rheumy water dripping from the trees, its tiny church one of the many buildings in Eden restored by Lady Anne. The church is kept locked to deter vandals, and I walked down to the post office to collect the key. The post office must be clinging on for survival by its fingertips, for it looks little used. Stooping beneath the door frame, I entered a bare room with a small, empty counter. The only adornments were an official notice hanging on the wall and a small paraffin heater. The postmistress, a kindly, grey-haired woman, hauled herself painfully through from the next room, her arthritic hips protesting at the exertion.

When I returned the key, after spending a few minutes in the simple, stone church, I remarked on the tapestry kneelers depicting local places and local people involved in the tasks of the farming year, lambing, clipping, hay-timing, gap-walling.

'They were done by a friend of mine, an old lady from Mallerstang. She died just after she finished them.'

We were joined by an old farmer calling in for a stamp and a chat. If Ben Alderson is a true descendant of the Norse, this man looked to owe his lineage to the Celts. His eyes were so dark they were almost black, his hair, once even darker, was now tinged with grey, and he was as short and stocky as a bull. We talked about the changes that had swept over Eden in the last few years, and I asked him if he could see a time when sheep farming might be driven out of the area altogether, caught between the hammer of the grouse moor owners and the anvil of the offcomers fuelling the house price spiral.

'People that breed sheep will be wanted yet a while, but things change. I would hope it doesn't, I mean, what else would you graze these hills with? You haven't a lot of alternatives on this sort of ground, unless you're going to turn to flower power like some over the top there.' His scathing reference was to the farmers of Swaledale, many of whom are now paid a grant by the National Park authority to restrict their use of fertilizers and delay their hay crop to allow the wildflowers and herbs in the hay meadows to thrive and set seed.

'Do you think the visitors realize how much the look of Eden owes to sheep farming, or do they think that it's natural, that it's always looked like this?'

'A percentage will realize well enough, and the rest will think it's just there, it's just happened, like, but it's farming keeps the landscape the way it is in these places. I mean, let it go wild into a wilderness, if it wasn't grazed and all the fences were down, it would soon look . . . well, nobody would want it, would they, like?'

# 4
# PENDRAGON TO NINE STANDARDS

Pendragon Castle

Shoregill, following a narrow, sunken green lane beneath a massive old sycamore, towards another of Lady Anne's restorations, Pendragon Castle. It scarcely survived her, and is now a hulk of crumbling masonry like a massive oak stump on the far side of the river, while a dead tree stands sentinel on the near bank.

The castle was the reputed home of Uther Pendragon, father of Arthur, but that must be taken on trust, for no trace of the Celtic stronghold remains. The stone castle dates from the eleventh century, when the chain throughout Eden was built at William Rufus's orders, to secure the North after his conquest of Carlisle. The Pendragon legend may well be as decrepit as the castle itself, for the name only came into use in the fourteenth century. Robert de Clifford took advantage of the medieval fascination with all things Arthurian to give himself a little extra social cachet by changing the name of his castle from the humdrum Mallerstang to the legendary Pendragon – a bit like the proud possessor of a semi-detached changing its name from Dunroamin' to Mon Repos, on the strength of a day trip to Boulogne.

Edward Baliol, King of Scotland, was entertained at Pendragon in 1333, but he cannot have been unduly impressed by his reception, for he returned to burn and destroy it during a border raid a few years later, one of several times that it suffered at the hands of the Scots.

Restored by Lady Anne Clifford, it was demolished by her successor and used, like Brougham and Brough, as a 'quarry' of dressed stones for his rebuilding at Appleby.

Enough remains to show what a stout, near-impregnable stronghold it was, its walls up to twenty feet thick and some forty feet high in places, dominating the valley and the river swirling by beneath its walls.

Crossing back over the river, I followed the narrow lane up a steep hill between hedgerows which are thick with summer wildflowers. At the top, a track led back towards the Eden. To one side is a limekiln, an ubiquitous sight in the high country, sited near an outcrop of lime and used to burn the stone, often with 'crow' coal mined from shallow drifts near the top of the fells.

The care with which even the most prosaic constructions, like these lime kilns, were built, is astonishing to me, an onlooker from the age of the breeze block. The corner stones are carefully dressed, the kiln mouth gracefully arched, all the more remarkable for the fact that most of the builders would not be craftsman masons, but local farmers.

The kilns are relics of the days when farmers burned their own lime for their fields and when many miners and small-holders would claim a small piece of 'intake' land along the edge of the moor. It would be laboriously cleared of stones, which were used to wall it, and then limed heavily to bring it into good grazing condition, supporting a couple of beasts, or adding to the vital hay crop. Now, most of the intakes are long abandoned and reverting steadily to moorland, with rushes and coarse grasses invading from the adjoining fell, and if a farmer needs lime for his land, he gets it from a plastic bag.

Across the river I could see a farmhouse standing in the shadow of a clump of Scots pines, memorials to the droving age, when two or three were planted as a sign to drovers and pack-horse trains far across the fells that food and shelter for the night could be obtained there.

The character of the valley had changed during the walk from Pendragon, the rugged high country left behind for the gentler, rounded contours of the mature Eden. Though still young, the river is already broader, quieter, its flow less troubled by rapids.

Climbing up the shoulder of the hill, beneath the limestone crags of Birkett Common, the ruins of Lammerside
Castle come into view. It appears to be on the far bank of the
river, but the Eden curves back on itself below the hill on
which the castle stands. Like Pendragon, or for that matter,
like the ruins of Ireland, another rain-washed land, there is an
almost organic feel to the castle remains, growing out of the
earth and slowly returning to it.

I approached the mound of crumbling masonry along an
avenue of nettles, the ruins part-covered by sprouting saplings
and clinging vegetation. Pennant, passing by in 1801, described it as 'a very ancient tower called Lammerside Hall,
known formerly as the Dolorous Tower'. The reason for that
sad soubriquet is unknown, and Lammerside will carry the
secret to the grave when the earth and vegetation finally
swallow it up.

I crossed the ploughed and re-seeded fields behind the
castle, the monotonous green of rye grass a dull contrast to the
herb and flower-rich hay meadows of the upper dale, and
followed the river on towards Wharton Hall, built as a larger
and perhaps more secure dwelling than Lammerside when the
Whartons abandoned it in the fourteenth century.

The river bank between the remains of the two ancient
monuments is studded with the detritus of life on a modern
farm: rusty wire, plastic fertilizer bags, even a discarded
television set. The bank is also punctuated by a remarkable
number of rusting cars, though these are not so much examples
of the farmers' cavalier attitude to waste disposal, as of
defence, the cars holding the bank against the relentless
erosive power of the river. The same function is performed
more naturally and far more elegantly by the roots of trees and
hedges, many of which have perhaps been removed by these
same farmers in their desire to squeeze every last ounce from
their land.

Two farm buildings from very different ages screen
Wharton Hall from view on the approach up a long concrete
drive: a huge, new, steel-frame building, succeeded by a stone

60

barn curving around the hill like a medieval fortification. The slits in its walls have the air of embrasures for archers, though their true purpose is a more prosaic one, to provide ventilation for the hay stored inside.

The gatehouse of Wharton Hall is a massive stone block, a pele tower solid enough to deter all but the most determined Scots marauders. The coat of arms of the Whartons is carved in stone above the entrance arch, which is 24 feet through, and the walls that remain are perhaps half as high again, with stone towers guarding the courtyard. It was described in 1777 as 'now in ruins and desolate, inhabited by no human creature but a poor hind'. Part of the Hall is restored and lived in now, however, and the sprawl of buildings around it suggests that the farm is far from impoverished today.

Walking down the track away from the Hall, I passed an old, gnarled oak, almost as broad as it is tall, with dead branches jutting out at all angles from its venerable bole. It must have stood there longer than the Hall itself. A Second World War pillbox squats on the skyline, beside the railway track, sentinel against the perils of a later and even darker age.

Different defences were required against a more recent threat to the railway, that of closure, which has hung over the line for twenty years. There may never have been a genuine economic case for the Settle–Carlisle line, which only came into being as the result of a misguided piece of brinkmanship by the Midland Railway. The arguments about its economics today remain as heated as the boilers on the steam trains that used to travel the line and as impenetrable as the smoke they left hanging in the long tunnels through the Pennines, but in a civilized country, the arguments would not be all about economics. The Settle–Carlisle is perhaps the outstanding monument to Victorian vision, determination and engineering skill. As one critic of the closure plans remarked: 'Hadrian's Wall and Durham Cathedral are not required to justify their existence on economic grounds, nor should the Settle–Carlisle.'

Prior to the building of the line, the Midland Railway's track ended at Tebay, in a junction with the London and North

Western Railway, who refused to provide connecting services to the North. The Midland began surveying the Settle–Carlisle route in 1865, and a bill passed through Parliament two years later. The Midland probably only intended to put pressure on the LNWR to come to terms, and the two companies soon reached agreement, subject to the Midland abandoning the line. When the Midland went back to Parliament with an abandonment bill, however, it was rejected and the company was compelled to construct the line. Not a single Eden Valley landowner had opposed the building of the railway, and over sixteen hundred signed a petition urging Parliament to reject the abandonment.

The line was built through some of the most difficult terrain and in some of the most intractable conditions that could be found anywhere in Britain. It was completed in only six years, but the cost in both financial and human terms was huge. The price to the Midland was 3.5 million pounds, a prodigious sum in Victorian England and more than twice the original estimate. The cost to many of the six thousand men who built the line was their lives, either from accidents or the typhus and cholera that swept through the shanty town construction camps, built on the open fells. The cemetery at the tiny church of St Leonard in Chapel le Dale, near the spectacular Ribblehead Viaduct, bulges with the railway dead.

Construction went ahead in the face of appalling difficulties: peat bogs that swallowed thousands of tons of rock for embankments without trace, landslips, mudslides, atrocious winter weather and winds so strong that some workers were literally blown over viaduct parapets. One newspaper correspondent sent to investigate the cause of delays in construction had this answer to critics: 'Let them go over it in the drenching rain of October, or let those who complain of its slowness in the making, wade through the mire, clay and water and see the slurry slipping away from the metals and add to these difficulties the cuttings through boulder clay and rocks of excessive hardness, the roving habits of the workmen and the wild inhospitable district through which it passes and then the wonder will not be that the works are incomplete, but at the possibility of completing them at all.'

The first passenger train ran in 1876. In Appleby they declared a public holiday and rang the church bells to celebrate a day that they, and many others in Eden, felt would be the beginning of a new era of prosperity, with the markets of industrial Yorkshire, Lancashire and Scotland at last open to them. That belief was not shared by the railway company, however, who saw the line simply as an improved express route into Scotland.

The wishes and needs of the local inhabitants have remained bottom of the scale of priorities of those running the railway ever since. The nadir was reached with the closure of all the stations between Settle and Carlisle except Appleby.

In the last few years, the line has seen a revival of passenger traffic, with several small stations re-opening. It is well-used by local people as well as tourists, but though it is now officially reprieved, a lingering doubt about its future remains. Some railwaymen claim that the line has been marked for closure since the end of the Second World War; certainly the pressure has been growing over the last twenty-five years. In theory it is now safe, as British Rail have lifted the threat of closure; in practice its long-term future remains as unpredictable as the Eden weather, but to close the line, or allow it to decay beyond recall, would be an act of public vandalism that our descendants would find hard to understand or forgive.

Local opinion is solidly in favour of its retention, even amongst the farmers who regularly lose stock, killed by trains after straying on to the track. I had talked to Ben Alderson about the railway, while sitting out the snowstorm up at his farm a few weeks before. He suffers more losses than most, but said: 'It would be a shame if it had to close, the work that's gone into it, and it would be hard work in them days. It's rather a liability at the moment, though, because the fences are bad at both sides. If you've sheep on it, you can get a lot killed. We had three rams killed on it last summer.'

'I've heard stories about farmers dropping dead lambs

over the fence on to the railway at night, so they can claim compensation; what about that?'

He grinned at me. 'You listen to too many stories. No, I don't think so, there wouldn't be a lot of that goes on. The railway might maybe think so, but we tend to do more fencing on that stretch than ever they do, just to keep stock off, because if you relied on them, you'd wait for ever, like.'

Rooks spiralled their courtship flights in the faded blue sky above me, their harsh calls like a sarcastic mimicry of the bleating of lambs, as I crossed the fields back to the Eden, now flowing beneath a rocky overhang, the tree branches drooping to touch the water surface. The river carves weird shapes from the rock as it drops towards the narrow gorge of Stenkrith, a frightening sight when in flood. Huge slabs of rock lie stacked up by previous floods and the river finds its way through strange, water-carved channels, with pillows of foam eddying out of the current. There are no jagged edges in this landscape; everything is worn, smoothed and rounded, not splintered by ice or wind, but ground down and water-cut.

As it passes beneath the arch of an old railway bridge, a relic of the Stainmore line, closed over thirty years ago, the river is compressed into a torrent, boiling down through the jaws of a rocky chasm, only inches wide. It is claimed that a local blacksmith once spanned the river here with his hand, then broke a piece of rock with his hammer to prevent anyone from repeating the feat. It would need a giant's hand to span it now, though it would be a comfortable step across, but for the slipperiness of the rocks and the sight of that ferocious force of water surging through the gap. The water is icy cold and so clear that I could see leaves swirling in the current, feet below the surface.

The river continues to run fast down through Stenkrith Park, flowing past a huge metal tank lying like a beached submarine on the river bed, another relic of the old railway, used when water was pumped from the Eden to refill the boilers of steam trains embarking on the viciously steep ascent of Stainmore.

The path emerges from the park into a series of pocket-handkerchief landscapes, vignettes that would haunt the sleep of expatriates in dry and dusty foreign lands. A pale sun shines its milky light on a soft, water-filled land. The river flows through deep pools beneath the shade of the trees, rising fish sending slow ripples across its surface. Cows stand passively in the shallows. The only intrusions into this bucolic idyll are sounds; the lorries grinding up to the quarry on Hartley Fell or the dull, sinister thud of explosions from the Warcop army ranges.

A path branches off up the hill, leading to Hartley village and the fells beyond. At the top of the moor, where Eden ends and the peat hags stretch away unbroken into the haze to the East, are the Nine Standards. The name may derive from their resemblance to 'standers', the pillars of rock left in coal mines to support the roof. From a distance they appear monolithic, but they are actually drystone stacks. Their purpose is unknown; some claim they were built to appear like an advancing army to marauding Scots, which suggests a contempt for Scottish intelligence that even the English would find hard to maintain.

The theory that they were boundary markers seems equally implausible – why build nine where one would do? Probably they were simply built by shepherds with time on their hands. Nine Standards has been a place where shepherds from either side of the fells have met for centuries to exchange stray sheep. Since building cairns on hills is an apparently elemental human need, as the heaps of stone every few hundred yards of the Pennine Way testify, perhaps the Nine Standards are simply cairns, built, for once, by men skilled in drystone walling.

# 5
# KIRKBY STEPHEN, STAINMORE AND BROUGH

Nine Standards

roof-tops of Kirkby Stephen, the capital of the upper Eden,
appeared among the trees. Stenkrith marks the end of the
river's youth; it makes one last flourish as it drops over some
rapids, then flows quietly down under the seventeenth-century
Franks Bridge. The Eden has become a sober, respectable
river, showing impeccable taste and discretion in slipping
quietly by behind the back of Kirkby Stephen, invisible and
unsuspected from the single, straight main road that runs
through the town. It doesn't intrude, for it knows its place,
essential behaviour in a sombre, staunchly 'chapel' town;
though the Eden's chosen course around Kirkby Stephen also
brings to mind Ruskin's remark that the retreat of glaciers is not
necessarily connected with the vulgarity of the tourists visiting
them.

The ever-present gathering of ducks beneath the old
pack-horse bridge set up a cacophony of appeals for bread as I
crossed the river and climbed Stoneshot, the winding lane
leading to the town. So narrow is the high-walled lane, that a
local legend, an essential part of the upper Eden apocrypha,
claims that two of the local salmon poachers, fleeing from the
long arm of the law, escaped by hurtling down Stoneshot in
their Mini. The pursuing police, based in Penrith and lacking
essential local knowledge, tried to pursue them in their patrol
car and found themselves wedged between the walls, unable to
go forward or back, or open the doors. Such a good story cannot
possibly be true; nonetheless, it provides a happy thought to
speed the journey up the hill.

Kirkby Stephen is a strange mix of a town with the feel of

an overgrown village, taking its physical shape and what importance it possesses as much from being on the road to somewhere else as from what it is in itself. Though the town lies on the important route up the Eden Valley to Carlisle, down the centuries it was always overshadowed by its near neighbour, Brough, whose massive castle dominates the strategic junction of that route with the road over Stainmore from Scotch Corner, the main road from London to Scotland from Roman times until the recent past.

I love the bleak, elemental desolation of Stainmore, but I can understand those who find its charms elusive. Sir Daniel Fleming, an eighteenth-century traveller, described it as 'high, hilly and solitary country, exposed to wind and rain, which, because it is stony, is described in our native tongue as Stanemoor, over which a great but no good road, the Post passing every week between Burgh and Bowes, and the coaches going often that way, though with some difficulty and hazard of overturning and breaking'. Two contemporaries, Nicolson and Burn, were even less complimentary: 'The badness of the road (which perhaps was indeed the worst hard road in England) contributed to render all the rest more dismal, and in stormy weather it was the more vexatious as the traveller could make no speed.'

Bad as the road was, 'fit only for a goat to travel', as long as it retained its importance as the major artery between London and Scotland, Brough continued to thrive on catering to the foot, horse and wheeled traffic travelling along it, which was perhaps just as well, for the wool from the local sheep was once described as 'the worst wool within the realm'.

The coming of the railways heralded Brough's ultimate decline. By 1860 it was described as 'little more than a village, the railway having destroyed the coaching trade which it formerly possessed'. The railways swept well wide of Brough, but passed within range of Kirkby Stephen, which expanded as Brough sank into obscurity. Its importance as a centre for trading livestock went into parallel decline, with Kirkby's Luke Fair replacing Brough Hill as the mecca for cattle and sheep sales, while Appleby inherited Brough Hill's horse trade.

Even when the importance of the railways grew less, Kirkby benefited from the expanding motor trade, particularly the charabancs taking a tide of workers from the North-east to Blackpool. I first encountered the extraordinary phenomenon of a Geordie homecoming from Blackpool on a late night drive from Scotland back to my home in Yorkshire about ten years ago. All good Cumbrians are normally safely tucked up in bed with a cup of malted milk and a digestive biscuit by half past ten at night, and I had seen scarcely a light since leaving Carlisle.

Entering Kirkby at one in the morning, I was astonished to find the town brightly lit and awash with people and traffic. At that time a café in Kirkby Stephen was close to the proverbial licence to print money, and the whole town stayed wide-eyed and occasionally legless until three in the morning, its plethora of cafés doing a roaring trade victualling the convoys of coaches bringing tired and emotional Geordies home from the Blackpool Illuminations.

Now Kirkby has slipped back into a deep Cumbrian torpor. The coaches no longer stop there, preferring fast food in a motorway service station to the uncertain reception of a town which is no longer sure it wants them, for Kirkby is increasingly a place with inhabitants as old and greying as its buildings. Many would like to see a bypass take the traffic for Blackpool and the Lakes away from the town altogether, leaving it to its auction mart and its strictly local trade, though the mausoleum air of the once-bustling Brough might give them pause for thought. A few years ago, you had to make an appointment to cross the road, so heavy was the flow of traffic. Now it hurtles along the new bypass with scarcely a backward glance, leaving Brough high and dry, like flotsam left by a receding wave.

The town's inordinate number of pubs and former pubs testify to its previous importance as a halt for travellers, but now it is a place where sleeping dogs not only lie, but do so in the middle of the road, at little peril to themselves.

Brough also has a bit of the grim air of a garrison town, perhaps unsurprisingly, since it grew up around a Roman camp and a Norman castle, and has virtually never been out of the sight of armed men in its history. Even now, the army is a constant, audible presence just along the road at Warcop. The medieval village, Church Brough, huddles between the castle and the church, which stand on separate mounds beyond Swindale Beck, aloof from the present town.

Behind its quiet, occasionally forlorn exterior, however, there is a lot of character to be found. If Kirkby Stephen is Cumbrian respectability cast in stone, Brough has a bit of a Wild West feel to it, a touch of lawlessness – what Cumbrians call 'rogueing'. There is even the occasional fist fight, though that isn't necessarily too surprising, given the potentially explosive cocktail of alcohol, young farmers, local girls and visiting 'squaddies' from the army ranges.

The pubs are much improved now, compared with a few years ago, when the 'B' in Brough pubs was definitely mute. The owner of Brough's night spot used to have a simple method of keeping order in those troubled times. As I was enjoying a drink there one Saturday night, a fight broke out, a by no means unknown occurrence. With practised ease and an air of indifference, the owner simply switched all the lights off, plunging the windowless room into darkness. Only those in direct physical contact with their opponents could continue to fight, and after a short cooling-off period, which I took the precaution of sitting-out under my table, still clutching my drink, the lights went back on, the music re-started and everyone carried on with their evening.

Long after the coaching age, the road over Stainmore continued to be a provider of sorts, particularly before it was improved, when lorries would frequently turn over on the icy bends, spilling their loads to provide winter pennies from heaven for Brough. The word would quickly be out around the town and, like Cornish wreckers, the locals were off up the hill, collecting whatever came their way. Salt, fresh herrings, washing soda, flat caps – 'there are still a few around', according to my informant, who, for the sake of decorum, I'll call William Ford – were among the booty, but their greatest haul rivalled that stripped from the SS *Cabinet Minister* in Compton Mackenzie's *Whisky Galore*.

I asked him if they ever got anything really valuable.

'To tell you the truth we did, aye. The best of the lot was a load of whisky. The wagon tipped over on that bad bend up towards the Punch Bowl. We got the driver away to a farm for a cup of tea, he wasn't really hurt, just shaken up a bit, and we got amongst it double quick. A hundred proof whisky for export, it was, beautiful stuff. There were a good few bottles smashed on the road, but we had plenty to go at. It was hidden all over the spot – hay barns, milk churns, hen houses, you name it. The police made a bit of a show of searching for it, but they knew they were on a loser, so they just did enough ratching about to keep their bosses happy and then gave up. I wouldn't be surprised if a bottle or two didn't go their way as well.' Lorries snowbound up on Stainmore still offer tempting targets, but the police now often mount guard, especially on valuable cargoes.

The Stainmore railway was the source of a few windfalls of a rather less providential nature. 'The bloke who operated the signals at Stainmore Summit had a couple of sons. They'd go down to the goods yard at Barnard Castle during the day and see what the train was carrying, then he'd stop it at the signal when it came up that night and the lads would be in amongst it, helping themselves to whatever they fancied.'

The great local pastime, however, undoubtedly was, and perhaps still is, poaching. 'When the Stainmore railway was open, you'd sometimes see a couple of grouse feathers sticking to the telegraph wire up above the railway line. If you looked around, there would be a dead grouse lying somewhere around there. We used to sit in the cabin up at the summit and pot grouse with an air rifle as well, and we would shoot them up on the moor with rifles, or sometimes net them. The net was laid flat during the day, at night we'd raise it on poles and then go round the moor driving the grouse into it.'

William had promised to tell me a few poaching tales and teach me how to tickle trout, and he led me out along the bank of the River Belah away from the Eden, heading up to one of his favourite spots for fish, on Argill Beck.

He quickly spotted a trout keeping station in the current close to the bank, and issued me with my deceptively simple-sounding instructions: 'Just tickle along under it until you get to the gills, then stick your fingers into the gills and flick it out.' I lay down on the bank, inching myself forward with the stealth of a commando approaching an enemy position, slid my hand into the water and, waving my fingers in what I felt was a passable imitation of a few strands of weed, I moved my hand towards the trout.

At the first touch of my fingers on its flanks, it took off as if hit with an electric cattle prod. Clearly my technique required a little polish. I tried twice more in the course of our wanderings that day and failed ingloriously both times, though perhaps I should not have been too surprised. My lack of manual dexterity is such that it usually takes me three attempts to tie my shoelaces.

William had watched my bungling efforts with a mixture of amusement, exasperation, resignation and despair. 'If you'd been here in the hungry times, the nineteen-thirties, you'd have starved to death within a week,' he said, taking over the tickling duties and promptly plucking out a plump brown trout with nonchalant ease. I sighed and resigned myself to the role of Boswell to his Johnson.

'Trout are fine for eating, but salmon were the way to make a few bob. Everybody used to be out after a salmon or two when they were running, you could take them easy with a torch and a gaff. We'd use one of them carbide headlights off a motorcyle – damn good lights. We'd take one of them, shine it on the water, just wiggle a gaff along under the salmon and then – phtttt! Argill Beck was a good spot, we used to get them down below the waterfall, just along there. By day you could use one strand off a rabbit snare. Clear water and very sunny, you'd just loop it over them until it got to the gills and then click!'

'You can do the job with salmon roe too,' said William, though it's an awful job to get it done right. They all have to be pricked and salted. We would go up stream a bit, lay a handful of roe on a flat stone and put another stone on top, so that the taste would drift down the stream. The trout would follow it up and we'd have a roe on a hook and just pull them out. Then we'd have a pod net, a big round net lying on the stones and we'd just flick it up, or you can use Domestos, it's like lime, it takes the oxygen out of the water.'

I wondered what the river bailiffs were doing while all this was going on.

'There were always plenty of bailiffs around, but one of them was very well in with a local man, he'd turn a blind eye. It was arranged between them that the local man would take salmon and flog them to the railwaymen down at Tebay.'

'But didn't anyone ever get caught?'

'Aye. There's a few lads that have been caught for poaching over the years . . . and a few that hasn't been. Years ago it was a bit of fun, but now the fun's gone out of everything.'

The fun involved everybody from the highest to the lowest. The Cumbrian poet Norman Nicholson used to tell a tale of a salmon poacher who was complimented by a friend on his good fortune after the chairman of the local bench of magistrates had taken pity on his plight and paid the fine he had imposed from his own pocket. 'So he bloody well should,' said the poacher, 'it was him that got the salmon.'

If it was partly fun, however, poaching was often a matter of necessity as well. As we walked across the fields away from the river, rabbits scattered before us, prompting William to reminiscence about older, harder times.

'In the Thirties and Forties, farmers made the rent from rabbits; cattle and sheep were worth nowt. If it hadn't have been for rabbits we'd have hungered. 1926, when the strike was on, it was hell, there was nothing. We managed to get a few rabbits and hares and my mother used to jug them the old-fashioned way. By, they were good.'

On the way back down to Brough, we talked of one other link with the past, Brough Hill Fair. Held since the thirteenth century, and once the biggest horse fair in the North of England, it is now close to moribund. A nineteenth-century document described the men, 'more developed physically than mentally', who had the dubious privilege of trying to get a halter on to the wild, unbroken fell horses known as 'stags', which were rounded up and driven down to Brough Hill to be sold.

Brough Hill, like Appleby, was a magnet for gypsies, who have always been heavily involved in horse-dealing, though it is clear that they were no more trusted in the past than they are in the present. An ancient rule, still in force, states that gypsies have to be off Brough Hill by noon of the day following the Fair, and across the county boundary before nightfall. The crowds that thronged Brough Hill were also irresistible to pickpockets and thieves. Those that were caught were held in the stone lock-up, which still stands in the corner of a field.

William had few complaints about the gypsies, however. 'There was always a bit of thieving when the gypsies were about, but it wasn't necessarily always the gypsies that were doing it. There were a few bad lots amongst them, but that's like any group of people, isn't it? I think the gypsies got badly liked when quite a number of a bad type – the Irish would maybe call them tinkers – came over and got them a bad name. Most gypsies, if you're straight with them, they'll be the same with you . . . mind you, they want watching if you're doing a deal!

'A few were a bit dirty and smelly like, but I got to be good friends with some. Things have changed now, though. There's one bloke who comes geared up like a gypsy to Appleby, but he runs a night club in Leeds, so he tells me. He still trades in horses when he comes every year, though. I think he just gears up for the occasion. He's naturally bred from that type of people, you can tell by the look of him.'

While Appleby Fair remains a great attraction both for

gypsies and tourists, no crowds now flock to Brough Hill, a far cry from the time when, as Addison writes in *English Fairs and Markets*, 'For days before the Fair was held, strings of ponies were to be seen along every road and green track, trotting towards Brough, as well as great herds of Scots cattle drifting slowly down from the Highlands.'

In the middle of the eighteenth century as many as 100,000 beasts would change hands each year at Brough Hill, most brought hundreds of miles in droves from the Highlands of Scotland. The droves, led by highly skilled drovers, took the most direct route, crossing the high moorland and averaging only ten to fifteen miles a day.

'They are required to know perfectly the drove roads which lie over the wildest tracts of the country and to avoid as much as possible the highways which distress the feet of the bullocks and the turnpikes which annoy the spirit of the drover; whereas on the broad green or grey track, which leads across the pathless moor, the herd not only move at ease and without taxation, but, if they mind their business, may pick up a mouthful of food by the way.'

Sir Walter Scott's view of a mouthful of food in *The Two Drovers* clearly does not quite match that of R. L. Stevenson, who complained in *St Ives* that 'a continual sound of munching and the crying of a great quantity of moor birds accompanied our progress, which the deliberate pace and perennial appetite of the cattle rendered wearisomely slow'.

Most of the great drove roads were originally established by the movement of stolen cattle, from which the Highland drovers also acquired their expertise. Rustling was practically the national sport in Scotland, and cattle were one of the most negotiable forms of currency; in the Highlands even the rent was fixed in terms of cattle. England provided an insatiable market for salt beef to feed the forces of the expanding Empire, and the Highlands were ideal for rearing, but not for fattening stock. The drovers were the link that bridged hundreds of miles of wild country, bristling with robbers and rustlers, bringing the stock to a market such as Brough Hill, from where a purchaser would be reasonably confident of getting home unmolested.

Improvements in transport and agriculture and the loss of more and more rights of 'passage and stance' across the uplands eventually killed the droving trade, however, and with it died Brough Hill, though a small, sad remnant still lingers on.

'Last year it was wet,' said William. 'It usually is, mind; Brough Hill weather we call it, but there were only thirty or forty people there. There used to be cattle, sheep and horses, and cheapjacks by the score, lining the road for quite a distance. Gypsy women were there every day, selling bits of lace, clothes pegs and all sorts, telling fortunes. At night they'd dance on the road. It was nearly as big as Appleby Fair, even then, but Appleby's got bigger and Brough Hill smaller. There was a bus every half hour out to Brough Hill, there's hardly a bus to anywhere now.'

Kirkby Stephen's equivalent, Luke Fair, has been held on 27 October, St Luke's Day, since a charter granted by Edward I in 1302. Pens full of animals once lined the streets, and pigs and poultry were sold from the back of farmers' carts, while cheapjacks and traders jostled for space. The road to Nateby was known as 'tup hill' for that was where the tups – the rams – were sold, in deals sealed with a slap of the hand.

A Court of Piepowder, a corruption of the Norman phrase *pied poudre*, used to be held at the time of the Fair, dispensing summary justice amongst the dusty-footed pedlars, broggers (wool buyers), badgers (pedlars of corn and general goods), salters, carriers and the other itinerant traders who thronged the streets.

Luke Fair was last held in the streets in 1941, but the Luke Fair sale in the auction mart is still the highspot of the local farmers' year. Sheep have grazed the surrounding hills for centuries, and the Swaledale breed, with its distinctive white nose and black face, has been registered since 1919, but it has become increasingly popular for upland farms throughout Britain in the last thirty years, and as demand has grown, prices for the majestic tups have soared.

The first tup to make four figures was in 1954, when one sold for £1,800. The man who auctioned it, Harry, remembers it well. He has a fund of tales about the mart, laughing himself into a coughing fit over the exploits of the farmers, their cunning and their legendary meanness, but his jokes do not wholly conceal a deep affection and respect for them. 'The farmers gasped at the price, they thought one would never be worth anything of the sort again, but prices have gone up ever since and the record now stands at £30,000.'

Though prices have genuinely risen to record levels, the price bid is not always what it seems, for 'luck money' can play a big part. In the old days, a luck penny was handed over to seal a deal, a practice similar to the acceptance of the King's shilling when joining the army, though there was also a superstition in livestock dealing that handing back a penny would make the animal lucky.

It is a tradition, like much else in upper Eden, that dates back to the Norse, who believed that luck was something that could be transferred through an object or in return for a gift. The luck of Edenhall, associated with a glass goblet, is one of several 'lucks' associated with places in Eden. Luck money has traditionally also changed hands in exchange for any sharp-edged gift, like a knife.

'There has always been a luck penny,' said Harry, 'but now pennies have got to be pounds. I think it's a bit to do with reputation. Some of these high prices are caused by jealousy; if your tup makes a thousand quid, maybe I'd want mine to make a thousand too, so I might offer a fair bit of luck money back.' Certainly there have been rumours of as much as one third luck money being handed over on one or two deals, and it is not too hard to believe them, for, like their sheep, hill farmers are a proud breed. To be seen to be bested by a rival in front of all your peers would be hard to bear.

Pride can be even more expensive to a farmer than that, however. The top prices are paid for the 'shearling' tups, the previous year's tup lambs, which are sold on their looks and pedigree, rather than on their performance, since as shearlings they have yet to sire any lambs. Tales are told of farmers paying huge prices for tups which either fail to show the proper interest in the job for which they have been bought or which produce poor offspring. Rather than admit the failure, it is claimed, some farmers have shot such tups and sent them away with the 'knacker men', never to be seen or mentioned again.

One other noble tradition connected with luck money is that it needs to be spent. The last night of the tup sales is a raucous night in every pub for miles around. Farmers who, for the rest of the year, find it hard to bring themselves to pay for their own drink, never mind that of anybody else, can be seen banging fistfuls of notes down on the bar and buying drinks for the house. A great stillness lies upon the land the next morning, with scarcely a farmer to be seen.

The same scene is repeated in miniature every week on market day, when a modicum of drink will be taken, even by those farmers with no reason to celebrate. It is a deep-rooted tradition, for I came across an entry in a farmer's diary from the mid-nineteenth century, which suggests that only the mode of transport has changed: 'To market with the wool. We got overmuch ale. Brother Edmund fell off his horse and lamed his leg.'

Though farmers keep up the tradition every week, the last night of the tup sales is by far the biggest night of the year. 'I remember one time, we'd got finished off at the mart and I'd popped into the Pennine for a drink,' said Harry. 'Quite a few of the farmers would pop in there for a quick one or two after the sales, leaving their tups penned up in the mart. Well it got to about nine o'clock and the foreman came in to say there was a tup of one of the farmers still in the mart and he wanted to get home. The farmer just shouted, "Fetch it in here, then", and carried on drinking with his mates. I walked down with the foreman and we dragged the tup back up to the Pennine between us. He wasn't really keen to go in there, but we got him in somehow and one of the farmer's mates announced, "That tup doesn't look so cheerful, Jack." The last I saw, they were trying to get a bottle of Guinness down it to cheer it up.'

Another great event in the farming year, the agricultural hiring, continued as late as the nineteen fifties in Kirkby Stephen. Men and women would line up in the streets, chewing a straw or sticking one in their hat-band to show that they were for hire. A deal would be struck with an employer for a sum of money, plus the worker's keep, and the bargain was sealed with a coin which, in common with the luck money on livestock, would almost inevitably find its way into a publican's till.

Apart from the serious business of finding work, hirings provided one of the few social events in the drudgery of the agricultural workers' year. Some got drunk, some fought, some got married and some took the King's shilling and enlisted, often after indulging in one or more of the other activities. The drinking and carousing led to the hiring fairs coming under strong pressure from the Temperance Movement and from moral reformers, who argued, not without some justification, that unscrupulous employers were hiring young female servants with more than the normal agricultural duties in mind. Pimps and bawdy house keepers also found them a fruitful source of new recruits.

Though the long-term agricultural hirings largely died out between the wars, hirings for haytime continued until about thirty years ago. 'A lot of local people would hire the Irish at haytime. The same ones would come back year after year. There were still odd Irishmen coming over until the middle and late fifties, but that's all finished now.'

# ·$\mathscr{S}$PRING·

AS the days lengthen, each pale sunlit morning offers hope of spring; each squall of rain, sleet or snow mocks that hope. The fells remain empty, save for the sheep, browsing among the peat hags for the thin gleanings left from winter, and the grouse, keeping their eternal vigils amongst the heather.

Yet one morning, apparently no different from those before, with cloud still clinging to the fells like a cold, grey shroud, and rain stinging the slopes, a lapwing tumbles into the air from a patch of rushes, in a ragged flight across the fell. It is the first of the thousands of birds returning from the marshes of the Solway to their breeding grounds high in the hills.

If the lapwings – 'tewits' in the local dialect, in mimicry of their cry – signal the end of winter, it is the haunting, liquid call of the curlew that is the confirmation that summer is at last close at hand. That magnificent call and the curlews' soaring flight counterpoint the song of the skylarks spiralling upwards into the summer skies, and at dusk, as even the sheep still their bleating, the last sound as night falls is the call of a curlew gliding down the wind to land, its flight as smooth and graceful as the curve of its beak.

# 6
# EDEN JAYS

rare as a rainbow in the uplands. Except for a few spring weeks, the fells remain a muted range of greens and browns and the sky is more often grey than blue. The farmers dress in wool clothing, dyed dull, natural shades, and even the upland sheep are more grey-brown than white, except for the new-born lambs and the glaring fleeces of the just-clipped sheep in early summer. This muted colour range makes the dayglo hikers' cagoules stand out like electric shocks up on the fells, but even these pale beside the astonishing sights often to be seen around Kirkby Stephen.

I was leaning against a wall on a typically grey Cumbrian morning, day-dreaming and chewing absent-mindedly on a sandwich, when a scarlet slash of colour flashed over the roof-tops. My first thought was that it was a parrot, but since wild parrots are even more rare in England than the proverbial rocking-horse droppings, I filed it away as one of life's unsolved mysteries and was preparing to return to the ruminative destruction of my sandwich when the red flash returned.

This time I was quicker to react, to be rewarded with the unmistakable sight of a parrot disappearing from view. Clearly an escaped pet, I thought, resolving to avoid involvement in lengthy missing parrots reports to the local police by ignoring it. Just then, however, a pair flew over, squawking loudly, before also disappearing among the rooftops. I looked down, to meet the eyes of a couple of local farmers regarding me with sly amusement. Their faces were as old and wrinkled as their caps, but the eyes watching me were as keen as a winter wind. There is nothing a farmer enjoys more than the chance to 'work' a stranger by spinning an initially credible, but increasingly implausible yarn, so I tried to resist the temptation to ask for an explanation and went back to the sandwich.

The farmers waited impassively as my common sense fought an unsuccessful battle against my curiosity. 'What were those birds?' I finally enquired.

'Oh, they're jays,' one replied, with a ghost of a wink to his friend.

'Unusual colour for jays, red and gold,' I said, 'almost the colour of parrots.'

'Ah they're Eden jays, though,' said the second farmer, eager to claim a share of the credit when the story came to be retold to their peers in the local later on.

'Those will be the ones that eat the wild grapes you see growing around here, I suppose,' I said, determined to go down fighting.

'That's the trouble with townies,' one remarked triumphantly to the other, 'they can't tell the difference between grapes and gooseberries.'

'Nor jays and parrots,' said his companion, laughing loud enough to drown the noise of the parrots overhead.

I gave what I hoped was an enigmatic smile and returned to my sandwich, resolving to leave the solution of the avian mystery until I could obtain incontrovertible evidence from my own eyes. A couple of weeks later, on my return to Eden, my patience was rewarded when I saw a flock of parrots and macaws in the trees around a large house, a short way outside the town. I resolved to enquire within at the first available opportunity.

The parrots are obviously a matter of some local entertainment and not a little local pride. I too, since my first encounter with them, have grown to enjoy the spectacle of a stranger to the town, gazing up in jaw-gaping surprise, then looking furtively round to see if anyone else has noticed this extraordinary phenomenon.

I returned to the banks of the Eden over Franks Bridge, to a chorus from the semi-wild, semi-tame ducks lurking beneath it, and followed the river along the 'backs' of Kirkby Stephen, past a flat-roofed concrete cricket pavilion that looked as incongruous as a multi-storey car park in this far corner of Cumbria. Punctuating the steady drone of traffic from the main road, the cawing of the rooks and the babble of birdsong from the hedgerows, were the calls of birds that would give an unsuspecting ornithologist nightmares for weeks, for the calls of an endless variety of macaws, cockatiels and parrots came echoing from the aviaries and trees in the gardens of the house across the fields.

The house is an impressive Victorian gentleman's residence surrounded by fine beech trees, each of which contains an unusually large nesting box. In the gardens are aviaries full of both exotic species and local wild birds, availing themselves of the rich pickings to be had. There is also an indoor aviary for birds that feel the cold and for those that are sick or need hand-rearing.

The owner, Michael Parker, could only be an Englishman. He was born and raised with all the material advantages any man could wish, and lives the life of a gentleman farmer, with no apparent financial worries to trouble him, passing his time in a fine house in a beautiful and peaceful corner of the country. Despite these advantages, however, I sensed a certain sadness in him. He seemed a man isolated by his wealth and position, imprisoned by his shyness, able to express himself only to his birds, perhaps feeling closer to them than any other living thing.

His sandy hair was thinning and his eyes were soft, and sad, the eyes of a man too much alone. He had travelled abroad as a young man, but now seemed settled into the long autumn of his life in Eden, caring for his birds.

Michael Parker's youthful interest had been in butterflies, before a chance encounter set him on the way to his consuming passion for birds. His mother's labrador picked up a badly injured racing pigeon, 'and for the first time I saw beauty in a bird. I nursed it back to health, but my father told me I had to return it; it had a ring on its leg, so we knew how to contact the owner. I was heartbroken to give it back, but in gratitude the owner gave me some squabs, which I reared.'

After receiving a budgerigar as a gift, he kept and bred them for several years, but he was so upset when a weasel got into his aviary and killed thirty-five of them, that he transferred his affections to larger, more easily defensible birds from then on.

We walked out through the garden, with Michael identifying every bird and relating its history. His birds have all the home comforts that they could want, food is plentiful, nest boxes and shelter are provided and there are even heated shelters to keep out the Cumbrian cold, though these are little used, except by the few birds that cannot fly. The dazzling aerial displays over Kirkby Stephen are the result of his determination that his birds should live as natural and free-flying a life as possible. 'Birds should be encouraged to fly. If they don't, their flight feathers atrophy. I was given one that had been a pet all its life; it's twenty years old and can't fly, and since they can live to be a hundred, that seems a bad thing.'

He has lost remarkably few of his birds. 'How do you start them off free-flying,' I asked. 'Aren't you scared that they'll just fly off and you'll lose them?'

'Once a bird is in good "yarrock" – that's a falconry term for being in good health and the right weight to fly – I get them going. To start with they fly well without being too much in control; they don't know where they're going to land. I lose a few before they get to the stage of being able to land where they want, but no sensible parrot flies off deliberately, he won't want to leave a place where he's comfortable and well fed. The nervous birds are doubly difficult to get flying free. I let the hen go first and the cock keeps her around by calling to her. When she's got used to flying around and coming back for food – once a bird has had food once, she'll never forget where she got it – then I let the cock bird out.

'I lose more cockatiels than anything else. On their first flight they go spiralling up into the sky, literally out of sight. I have to keep stirring up the others, trying to make them call, which is what draws the other one down again, but I lose more of them than anything.

'I learn about their interrelationship from watching them free-flying. Three blue and gold macaws got too matey; like humans, two is normally company and three over-crowding. The three of them flew right to Newton Aycliffe in County Durham. It was a lovely spell of June weather, clear and sunny, with no wind. Two days later, two of them returned absolutely exhausted, it took another two days for them to recover.

'Two months after that I saw one advertised in a paper, which had been captured after it had crashed in a field of corn. I picked it up from over in Newton Aycliffe, thinking that if it was mine, it would recognize its home surroundings immediately. As soon as I released it, it flew directly to the very small exit from what is a very large aviary, so it was clearly the same bird. Someone else told me they had seen it at Scotch Corner.

'One green-wing macaw – they're notorious wanderers – took itself and five others to Bowes. The weather broke and we had nearly a complete white-out, but two days later, there it was, absolutely bedraggled, clinging to a tree in the garden. A friend had seen it up on Stainmore. It's pretty unique for them to come back from so far away: usually if they fly more than two miles, they're gone.'

'So like the sheep, your parrots are "heafed" to a Cumbrian fell-side?'

'I suppose they are.'

'Could they survive and become a permanent wild colony?'

'No, because the birds can't feed themselves the whole year round. I was worried by the provisions of the Wildlife and Countryside Bill, and I wrote to the Minister, but he wrote back to say: "Since your birds cannot survive for 365 days a year without being fed by you, it is perfectly legitimate to have them flying free".'

To my surprise, Michael said that his birds forage more successfully in winter than summer, for there are more fruits and berries for them to eat. He has two Indonesian King

Parrots, which can go missing for up to three months at a time, living on fruit, crab apples, hawthorn berries and the peanuts and fat put out for wild birds. Only in a really hard winter will the native birds, such as fieldfares, completely strip the hedgerows of berries.

As well as caring for his own birds, Michael is an inadvertent, but very willing feeder of the wild bird population. 'When the weather is bad there are literally thousands of wild birds flying into the aviaries to feed.' He also puts food out for the wild birds and has a conservation field and a lake, while owls and jackdaws take over the parrot nesting boxes. 'Lots of people try to encourage owls to nest, but I have two pairs of tawny owls that breed every year in my parrot boxes.'

He also unintentionally provides food for sparrowhawks, though they seem to prefer good, plain British food to a more exotic diet. The cockatiels have a one-way entrance hole to their aviary, for they have to be inside at night or the owls eat them, but one night a sparrowhawk got in as well. 'I heard terrible noises from them, but it hadn't taken a single one. They go into the big aviaries to catch the wild birds, though. I saw one take three wild birds once and then fly sluggishly away. I didn't like to watch without intervening, but I had to know, and hawks do only kill to eat.'

His aviaries have almost reached saturation point, but he still harbours an ambition to breed African grey parrots, although his hand-rearing imposes a strain. 'Hand-rearing is always the result of the same problem, breeding too late. They have to be fed twice a day from September to March. I had to go to hospital a few years ago, and my gardener, Arthur, saved Moses' life by feeding him while I was away.' Both Moses and Arthur are still thriving.

# 7
# WINTON AND BECKFOOT

Swaledale Tups

raucous call of a macaw, I walked across the fields towards
Winton, one of the many fiercely independent villages of the
upper Eden. The rivalry of these small communities has been
known to spill into violence in the past, though that is now
largely confined to the annual Waitby Cup, a football competition open only to the inhabitants of the upper Eden villages.

I was introduced to its bruising brutality while living in
the tiny, nearby hamlet of Rookby. Finesse and football skill
are all very well, but the Waitby Cup also requires a Pass-
chendaele-like willingness to go over the top, whatever the
cost in lives or limbs. After our local derby against Winton, I
could scarcely walk for two days, while my partner at full-back
had to be lifted into his tractor seat to do his daily work. Such is
the ferocity of the tackling that it is an unusual year in which
one or two legs are not broken along the way. I was almost
entirely bereft of footballing skill, but I launched myself at the
opposition with such gusto that I was threatened with post-
match violence by no fewer than three of them. Had a football
manager been watching, my whole-hearted commitment
would certainly have had him reaching deep into his store of
clichés. I gave 110%, and at the end of the day, that's what the
game's all about.

It was clearly a day for exotic birds, for amongst half a
dozen wild duck flighting up from a tiny stream in the corner of
a field on the outskirts of Winton was one absolutely pure white
one, a Moby Duck that would be fortunate to survive some
shotgun-toting Ahab in the wildfowling season.

Winton's charms are elusive to the walker approaching

from this direction. The first impression is of a huddle of large farms, composed of clusters of almost equally large farm buildings, from many of which comes the distinctive, and, at some times of the year, overpowering smell of silage. The smell also clings to the clothes and hair of those that work near it, and the entry of one or two dairymen into Winton's delightful pub can be detected by the nostrils as easily as the eye.

It was in the Winton pub that I suffered one of the more severe humiliations in a long line of largely unsuccessful attempts to interest the opposite sex in my manly charms. I had spent an evening indulging in authentically British male behaviour, drinking beer and directing long, meaningful looks, designed to showcase my brooding intensity, at a particularly beautiful woman across the room. The fact that she was sitting with a man friend was no obstacle to my increasingly inebriated attempts to establish eye contact. Reluctantly I decided that it was time to move on, but I paused at the top of the two steps leading to the back bar, to direct one last haunting look in her direction.

Unfortunately, in so doing, I missed the top step, stumbled and hit a farmer at the bottom of the steps squarely between the shoulder-blades. The impact caused him to fall against his companion, emptying his pint over her in the process. I watched, horrified, as the collisions and spillages spread outwards like ripples on the surface of a pool. Having replaced more drinks than could ever have been spilt in the human dodgems I had created – farmers may be slow talkers, but they are quick thinkers when the situation requires it – I left the pub with burning cheeks, a heavy heart and an empty wallet. I had never realized until then that the saying 'pride comes before a fall' was supposed to be taken literally.

Around Winton's tiny green are a number of typical Eden houses, the porous stone limewashed or, more commonly these days, pebbledashed, against the insistent Cumbrian rain, with the corner stones, lintels and window surrounds picked out in a contrasting colour. At the top of the village is a small common, where gypsies still camp every summer on their way to Appleby

Fair; close by is a pound where stray stock were once held, to be released only on payment for the grass and fodder they had eaten. Every village once had a similar common or goose green with a pond; these were ideal halts for gypsies, but most are now enclosed; from common land and rough grazing, the gypsy habitat has changed to industrial wasteland and scrap metal.

While I had been wandering across the fields to Winton, the Eden had been taking a different course. I set off in pursuit, strolling down the lane to Beckfoot, along a hollow way sunk four feet below the base of the hedgerows on either side. In a field off the lane were a group of Swaledale tups, more fortunate than the ewes, which remain on the fells throughout the winter.

The tups were wintering on good lowland grass, recovering from their prodigious exertions at tupping time. They are turned out to serve the flock on the same day every year, though that date gets later, the further up the fell-sides the farm is situated. The sheep are tupped at the time that ensures the earliest start to lambing after the worst of the winter weather is gone.

Most farmers keep diaries, recording the date when the first lamb was born, when the last snow fell, when the swallows returned, when haytime began and when it ended, sometimes months later. Through the recording of these dates, they may hope to reach a better understanding of the seasons and weather that govern their lives. Like the naming of every feature of their land, perhaps the numbering of all the events of their year gives them some power or imposes some order on the apparently random variations within the succession of the seasons.

Some dates in those diaries are as fixed and immutable as the bedrock of the hills, however. The date on each farm when the tups are turned out has not changed, perhaps for several centuries, certainly for as long as any of the farmers now alive can remember, although the unpredictability of the weather can often make a nonsense of these careful and long established plans.

This constancy is one of the enduring and endearing features of rural life. Come war, plague or famine, the tups will continue to be turned out to serve the flock, the lambs to be born, the sheep clipped and the hay crop cut and gathered, a sequence as unyielding as the natural cycle which dictates its course.

Great historical figures like Edward I, Robert de Brus, or even Lady Anne Clifford, may divert the course of history by their actions, and be celebrated long after their deaths as a result, yet there is as much quiet satisfaction in putting a tap root down to that constant natural sequence, flowing like the river through Eden. Those of us who live in towns and cities tend to sublimate that loss of contact with the natural cycle into obsessive gardening and fantasies about rural retirement, but even those who make the move to the country can find that there is far more symbolism than substance in the appeal of that kind of rural living.

My flippancy about my motives for moving to the pub on the hill concealed a real desire to become a genuine part of a rural community, living in it, working in it, giving to it, as well as taking from it. Although I had been living in rural areas for some time, I felt almost a parasite on the communities, living there but working elsewhere, doing work that was close to incomprehensible to the people I lived amongst. 'We get callouses on our hands, you get blisters on your backside,' as one farmer put it to me, not entirely in jest.

I wanted, quixotically, no doubt, to take up work that would involve me in the community and have a perceived value to my peers there. The pub seemed to fulfil those criteria. It conferred benefits, particularly those of late or occasionally all-night opening, and, just as important to a rural community, it was demonstrably hard work, involving long hours, some strenuous physical effort, and a measure of hardship in living on those exposed tops. I swelled with pride whenever a local confided to me, 'You wouldn't catch me living up there.'

So I tried it, and in some senses it worked. We were

accepted, though that owed far more to my wife's warm and outgoing personality than to any virtues of mine, but the quiet satisfactions of being a part of that community did not entirely compensate for a lack of challenge or mental stimulation in the work, nor for the sheer back-breaking drudgery of running a pub, particularly one open from what often seemed to be dawn to dawn.

'I'd love to retire to a country pub,' our unwitting tourist customers would say, as we exchanged looks varying from amusement to incredulity behind the bar. Yet even without the drudgery, there is a downside to the peace and tranquillity that make rural life so attractive – boredom. I can pause on the doorsteps of two or three Eden pubs and, before opening the door, predict precisely who will be in, what they will be doing, where they will be sitting, what they will be drinking, even what they will be talking about.

To people who feel trapped in a high-pressure, frenetic city life, the rural life can seem like heaven, but living in the midst of it in the depths of winter, with no strangers to enliven the scene, it can begin to seem more like hell. For every offcomer who settles for good in Eden, there will be another who stays a while, then packs up and moves on.

The resting Swaledale tups had no choice about their place of residence, but they and the young 'hoggs' – last year's lambs – which have their first winter in the lowlands before joining the breeding flock on the fells, were more comfortably off than their kin on the hills above.

Except for these privileged Swaledale tups and hoggs, the sheep grazing this low-lying land are the fat cousins of the hill sheep. The Suffolks and Leicesters that thrive down here could not survive on the coarse vegetation from which the Swaledales get their nourishment; life for man and beast is softer and easier here.

The lane was so quiet that one car would have been a surprise and two astonishing, but the quiet beauty of the landscape was marred by the thud of explosions from the Warcop ranges, now close at hand, though their grumblings echo from one end of Eden to the other. The whole of the valley, like rural areas everywhere in England, is marked by this intrusion of harsh twentieth-century reality into the pastoral idyll. Though the sound of explosions, the scars of mineral extraction and the sight of factories may distress the visitor, not to mention the retired couples who settle here in droves, they are music to those trying to earn a living here. 'You can't eat scenery' is a universal motto of areas of outstanding natural beauty.

That may not be entirely true, since the landscape cake can provide sustenance too. Instead of clipping sheep, farmers and others could try their hand at fleecing tourists, although jobs from tourism tend to be part-time, seasonal and slanted towards the female workforce, rather than the 'proper' jobs their men want. Whether every pound spent by the army in employing civilians on the Warcop ranges, may not be balanced by another lost, as a tourist or small business is driven away by the sound of guns, is an argument for the taproom regulars to consider in the long winter months. Certainly tourists must resent their peaceful country holidays being interrupted by the visible, and very audible practice sessions for the Third World War. Perhaps they would be less intrusive in a more generally noisy area, but here, where the sound of human voices can carry for a mile across the fields, the noise pervades the valley from Mallerstang almost to the gates of Carlisle.

Off to the side at the bottom of the lane is the attractive rambling farmhouse of Skelcies, a hotch-potch of buildings of different ages, all accreted together. It's a typical farmhouse pattern, with bits being added at either side as needed, though, in addition to the usual extensions at either end, one has also been built directly on to the front. Behind and to the left of the main frontage is what is clearly the original, far smaller farmhouse. It is built from the Eden stone, warm to the touch and glowing the colour of port wine in the rays of a setting sun. The old walls are smothered in lichen, in tribute to the fertility of the climate, and of the stone itself, which breaks down into the rich Eden soil at the fall of a raindrop.

# 8
# SOULBY TO APPLEBY

Green Lane

the Eden, across the fields from Beckfoot, but it was a fleeting reunion, for there are no rights of way within range of the river here. I crossed the narrow footbridge and followed the side of Scandal Beck, walking up the track towards Soulby, through the remains of the embankment of the Stainmore railway line. A derelict railway is always a sad sight, but this one reawakened thoughts of the similar fate that may one day await the Settle–Carlisle line.

I walked on, the mood of depression heightened by yet another mound of black-bagged 'big bales', but lightened by the sudden appearance of a jet-black horse looming up out of the mist. At the top of the track, I walked in towards Soulby, a neat village of traditional Eden stone houses and the increasingly prevalent pebble-dashed bungalows.

The unanimity of taste in rural areas separated by hundreds, and even thousands of miles is remarkable. The Tex-Mex, Ponderosa-style bungalow is as ubiquitous and apparently as sought-after by the farmers of England, Wales, Scotland and Ireland as it is by those of New Zealand, Australia or, indeed, the USA itself, and the same dreary whine of a pedal steel guitar and the voice of a lonesome cowpoke issue from their car radios all over the world.

Beyond Soulby, the Eden Valley is already beginning to assume the characteristics of its maturity and old age, now becoming such a wide valley that it almost ceases to qualify for the name. The land is flat or gently undulating, the flatness accentuated by the mist shrouding the distant hills from view. I trudged across fields full of glutinous mud that only hundreds of years of pouring rain, constant manuring and the treading of a million cows' hooves can achieve.

Past the farm of Ploughlands I climbed a green way, trapped between two hedges running straight up the hillside. It is astonishing how many green ways have survived, even in the lowlands, some with one of the walls or hedges removed, but others completely intact. In more intensively farmed areas, all trace would have been lost long ago, the hedges grubbed out, the walls removed, but here even those that no longer have a function tend to survive.

The narrowness of these old ways shows that their use was restricted to stock, men and pack-horses. No wheeled traffic would even attempt these muddy tracks, and they had only to be wide enough for a pack-horse carrying two panniers, or a farmhorse pulling a wooden sled, to pass.

Very few people possessed any kind of wheeled transport, even in the eighteenth century. As a writer of the time recalled: 'Only yeomen and the larger occupiers could boast of carts; the produce of the farms, hay, corn and peat, being brought in on railed sledges and the more portable articles on pack-horses. Coal and lime were conveyed by the last method across the miry moors and commons, where tracks instead of roads existed till near the end of the eighteenth century; and many persons now living remember the very common use of the pack-horse both as the general carrier from town to town and the vehicle in transit for grain to the mill or market and for manure, etc, on the farm.'

With transport only possible by pack-horse over these green ways, the price of a heavy commodity such as coal, lime or salt, a vital necessity at a time when the only way to preserve meat was to salt it, could double or treble in the space of a few miles. Struggling on foot along one of these green ways, once the prime arteries of trade, the true scale of the revolution in transport created by the development of turnpikes, canals and railways is brought vividly to life.

The green way leads into a rough stone track along the ridge, overlooking a small valley. Eden is actually a series of valleys, often very private, almost unknown and undisturbed. Small ridges and hills conceal a couple of farms, a few fields and a small beck, which briefly creates its own microcosm, before slipping down to merge with the Eden. These little side-valleys are remote now; in past centuries, even the few miles to Kirkby Stephen or Appleby must have seemed like a journey to the end of the known world.

The track dips, then runs along a scarp fifty feet above the river, the far bank more than usually dense with abandoned cars, an elephants' graveyard for old vehicles. The river runs fast along a natural stone pavement and, when it is not in flood, the great flat slabs of stone lie exposed like beached whales.

After a stretch of pleasantly unkempt oak, and then larch woodland, with great cushions of branches smothered in larch needles, I came out into the open, with the breadth of Eden spread out all around. The rich fertility of this riverside land must make farmers from the fell-sides weep with impotent rage at their own shallow, rain-leached and acid soil. I dropped down into Little Ormside past some of the fruits of that fertility, a huge clamp of silage under a black polythene sheet, weighed down by hundreds of tyres.

I delight in the ingenuity of farmers, lateral thinkers to a man, who can take such a quintessentially worthless object as an old tyre and put it to work. Their resourcefulness is exemplified in their multitude of uses for the ubiquitous baler twine, which can solve problems that would leave Einstein scratching his head. Gate hinges made from leather straps or the soles of old wellington boots, and redundant railway wagons pressed into service as moor-top hay barns, are further proofs of the farmer's ingenuity, but to me tyres are the ultimate testament.

To look on a pile of worn-out, useless, hideous tyres, impossible to destroy, give away or dump, and see in them a use that no one else has considered, requires the resourcefulness and cunning of a third world rag-picker or a farmer from any world. By contrast, my own inability to solve the simplest practical problem would even guarantee failure on a wheelbarrow maintenance course. Faced with a mountain of used tyres, my solution would have been to douse them in petrol, toss on a match and run like hell.

A farmer can tinker with a tractor, breathe life into a moribund hay-baler, build a shed, calve a cow or find a sheep in a snowstorm, but the divisions between man's and woman's work are so deeply ingrained that, asked to cook his own dinner, even the farmer's fabled ingenuity will not be equal to the task. When Ben Alderson's wife goes to Kendal to do the Christmas shopping, his neighbours send his meals round, ready-cooked, for without them he might starve. . . .

At the side of the track by Ormside Lodge, a circular pond pulses with a score of springs bubbling up, sending puffs of sand up into the clear water. In the garden is a magnificent Cedar of Lebanon, brought back from the Lebanon by General Whitehead. He grew the sapling in his hat and shared his daily one pint water ration with it on the long sea journey home.

I followed the lane down towards Great Ormside to the desolate accompaniment of rooks cawing from the trees. The fourteenth-century pele tower of Ormside Lodge loomed up to the right, beyond it the stepped roofline of the church and beyond that, in turn, the graceful arches of the Ormside viaduct of the Settle–Carlisle line.

I rested for a few minutes with my back to a sycamore tree growing out of the middle of some rough stone steps, beside the approach to the church. The sycamore has grown there for three hundred years, replacing the old market cross, which was destroyed in the Civil War. A cheese and butter market was held until well into this century. The market and the heavily fortified hall and church suggest that Ormside was once a far more important place than the sleepy village it has now become.

The church tower was clearly as much a temporal as a spiritual asset, for it provided a reasonably secure refuge from Scots raiders. The only entrance is from within the church, and a conical recess in the wall of the porch – an early equivalent of a fish eye in a house door – allowed the villagers in the tower to see their enemies without being seen. Even if the Scots managed to force their way into the main body of the church, they would not necessarily have been able to breach the door to the tower, for the defenders could fire down on them through embrasures high in the wall. The church stands on a semi-artificial defensive mound, in which relics of pre-Christian burials, a fine Viking sword and the Ormside Cup, a magnificent piece of Anglo-Saxon metalwork, were found.

A strange stillness drops on the land before rain. The birds stop singing and there is a soft expectancy, broken by the first few drops of rain. With an anxious eye on the darkening sky, and ignoring, with some reluctance, the call of the Hilton Arms, I followed the path away from the village, through the arch under the railway line, and across the fields to the steep and slippery Jeremy Gill. Quiet rain began to fall, scarcely hard enough to feel on the skin, but the misty, ceaseless rain that would soon soak me gently to the skin.

As I reached the top of a hill, near a massive oak tree surrounded by a copse of silver birch, the four turrets of Appleby Castle came into welcome view in the distance. I dropped down the bank to the riverside, and found the Eden still and quiet, the leaves floating all but motionless on the surface. Twenty or thirty ducks took off as I appeared through the trees, the water splashed like gunshot by their sudden flight.

As I approached Appleby, rough woodland gave way to parkland. The iron frames which had been placed around the young trees to protect them from grazing stock, fifty, perhaps a hundred years ago, were now deeply embedded in the bark. The turrets of the castle were hidden from view as I came out from under the lines of dripping trees, into a lane leading down to the ford across the river. Facing me, in the high perimeter wall, was an iron-studded door barring the way to the castle.

Appleby Castle stands on an almost perfect defensive site. The Eden doubles back on itself, guarding the castle hill from the north, east and west, while a stream through a marsh, Doomgate Sike, reinforced by a ditch and bank, provided some protection from the south. The streets giving access to the town, the Wiends, are narrow and winding, and were easily blocked and held against attackers. Even after breaching these defences, aggressors still had to contend with the castle walls and the solid Norman keep.

The castle occupied a key strategic position, dominating the Scots' main invasion route and threatening their line of retreat. As a result, both it and the town outside its protecting walls were repeatedly attacked. The Scots virtually destroyed the town in 1174 and 1314, while their regular raids for plunder kept the population in a perpetual state of terror. The Black Death added to Appleby's misery and the Crown was forced to grant the townspeople money 'in compassion of their impoverishment by pestilence, by removals and by the wars with Scotland'.

On St Stephen's Day in 1388 came the final blow. The Scots laid the whole town waste and it was never to recover from that devastation. Many were killed, many more ruined, and most of the survivors abandoned the town. Even today, over six hundred years later, the population of Appleby has yet to reach the fourteenth-century level. A visitor in 1515 wrote: 'The town has been set on fire and burnt by the Scots in the year of our Lord 1388, and never from that same time until now rebuilt, but the greatest part of the same town as yet lies in ruins.' Camden noted in his *Britannica*, almost one hundred years later: 'If antiquity did not make it the chief town of the County, and if the assizes were not held in the Castle, which is the public gaol for malefactors, it would be very little above a village.'

At about the time of Camden's visit, Appleby was hit by the Plague, which killed 128 people, perhaps as much as a third of the remaining population, while the remnants of the town took a further battering during the Civil War, the Royalist sympathies of the area not endearing it to Cromwell's conquering troops.

This was Lady Anne Clifford's inheritance, a region brought to its knees by ceaseless warfare and raiding, where scarcely a thought for the future had been possible for twenty generations. The landowners were absentees, interested only in squeezing the maximum rent from their long-suffering tenants, most of whom lived in poverty, despite the rich fertility of their land.

Lady Anne, disfigured by smallpox at the age of thirty-four, had fought to come into her inheritance for years. She was forced to battle with a succession of male relatives and with her husband, who sought to use her inheritance to settle his debts. Her determination was at last rewarded when, already well into her fifties, she finally inherited the Northern estates that she had scarcely even seen.

She survived for another thirty years, and in that time she transformed the upper Eden from a wasteland into an area of relative stability and prosperity. She rebuilt all her six ruined castles, and though an excessively romantic streak led her to restore them in out-dated medieval style, uncomfortable to live in and all but worthless to her successors, the work provided by the rebuilding was of lasting value to the population.

Her 'passion for bricks and mortar' also led her to restore churches and chapels, repair roads and build almshouses – still standing today and still occupied by elderly women of Appleby. She dressed in the cheapest, coarsest clothes, bought all her supplies locally and paid cash for them: habits almost unheard of among the nobility. She disbursed alms and generous charity to any who approached her gates, and became regarded as an almost saintly figure. This was all the more remarkable in view of the hatred with which her Clifford forebears had been regarded by the people of Eden. The Cliffords were notorious for their rack-renting and harsh treatment of their tenants, one head of the house of Clifford being described as 'in great danger of his life, for no man is worse beloved'.

Feelings ran so high over the extortionate policies of the absentee landowners that they spilled over into rebellion. The Pilgrimage of Grace, which swept across the North in 1536, though ostensibly inspired by the desire to restore the Catholic religion, was in fact much more concerned with the economic grievances of the suffering tenants. It began on the Clifford estates in Mallerstang and on Stainmore, where many new enclosures were destroyed, and swelled into an army that marched to the gates of Carlisle.

The leaders of the Pilgrimage allowed themselves to be soothed with vaguely worded promises from the King, Henry VIII, and encouraged their followers to disperse. The King's instructions for the punishment of the rebels indicate the value of his promises: 'Before you close up our banner again, you shall cause such dreadful execution to be done upon a good number of these habitants of every town and village that hath offended in this rebellion as well by the hanging of them upon trees as by the quartering of them and the setting up of their heads and quarters in every town great and small, which we require you to do without pity or respect.'

His Majesty's orders were carried out to the letter, despite problems in obtaining the necessary supplies: 'They shall be put to death in every town where they dwelt. Twelve of them here for the assault given to this city [Carlisle], and as many as chains of iron can be made for in this town and in the country shall be hanged in them, the rest in ropes. Iron is marvellous scarce.' Those people, usually the wives, who attempted to cut down the bodies to bury them, were hounded and persecuted.

Given this savage history, the people of Eden had no reason to love the Cliffords, but Lady Anne's building schemes, her fair dealings and her acts of charity swiftly won her tenants' loyalty and affection. Despite her generosity, however, she was far from a soft touch, and she was a ferocious defender of her rights, willing to go to extraordinary lengths to enforce agreements with tenants who presumed to avoid their due payments. The words 'Retain your loyalty, Preserve your rights', inscribed on the stone pillar, the High Cross, outside the castle gates, were both her own motto and her exhortation to her people. An indomitable woman, at different times she defied her husband, her king and even Cromwell, retaining her loyalty to the Stuarts and preserving her rights of inheritance.

As the visitor can read in the church of St Lawrence at the foot of the hill leading to the castle, she died on 22 March 1675, aged eighty-six, 'Christianly, willingly and quietly, havynge before her death seene a plentiful issue by her two daughters of thirteen grandchildren, and her body lyes buryed in this vaulte.'

# 9
# HIGH CUP NICK

High Cup Nick

psychological, if not quite the physical halfway-mark on my journey through Eden, I decided to reward myself with a detour to a spectacular natural feature, High Cup Nick, a deep fissure in the edge of the Pennines, with stunning views out over Eden. I had been following the valley floor since I came down from Black Fell Moss, and I had a hankering to walk some high ground for a while.

High Cup Nick and I had not enjoyed a happy relationship in the past, for twice I had been driven back while attempting to reach it, once by natural forces, once by the armed forces. My first ascent ended in ignominious failure a few hundred yards from base camp. Sue had dropped me off at the fell-side village of Hilton and gone to spend the day seeing a few friends, having arranged to collect me from the pub in Dufton after I had walked up to and around High Cup Nick.

I waved her off on a sunny, windless morning, perfect for a stroll along the tops, and set off up the track in high spirits. After four hundred yards, I came to a juddering halt at a barrier across the track. A red flag fluttered from a pole and a notice warned me that the firing ranges were in use, entailing deadly peril if I went further. I defiled the morning with a torrent of imprecations against firing ranges, armies, guns, overgrown boy scouts and freelance journalists foolish enough to let their transport disappear without first obtaining a contact number. Then I beat a retreat, spending the day wandering among the fellside villages, which was pleasant enough, but not quite what I had intended.

For my next attempt I took no chances, telephoning

ahead to make sure that the ranges would not be in use. Again Sue dropped me off, this time with our dog and my mate Pete for company, and the three of us set off boldly from Dufton for the hills. It was a close, overcast morning, with the clouds occasionally spitting a few drops of rain, but there seemed no great danger of any serious downpour, at least until we had climbed up past Dufton Pike, when we looked up to see the sky darkening and heard the first faint grumbles of thunder beginning to sound over the hills to the north.

'What do you want to do?' said Pete.

'Let's go on, it probably won't be much of a storm. It might even pass us by altogether.'

We carried on, past the old mines, intending to walk round by the tarns on the top of the moor, so that we would first see High Cup Nick from its most impressive side, looking down the deep natural cleft towards Eden, far below. We were squelching our way across the moor when it began to rain, hard.

'Might as well carry on – even if we go back, we'll still get wet,' I said brightly, buttoning my coat.

We splashed on over the moor, enduring the reproachful looks from an already bedraggled dog. Thunder had been rolling around the edge of the hills for some time, but now the storm moved towards us. Its timing was perfect. We were at the farthest possible point from both Dufton and Hilton, in the middle of a featureless moor without even a rock for shelter, exactly halfway between the tracks along Great Rundale Beck and High Cup Nick.

Thunder was now roaring every few seconds, lightning forking into the fells around us and rain pummelling down on us. An upland farmer would have described our situation as 'just fair', though we could have found far more explicit terms for it. The dog was doing her best to burrow into a stream bed to get away from the noise, the lightning and the torrential rain, and I was sorely tempted to join her.

We abandoned any thoughts of reaching High Cup Nick and beat a painfully slow retreat from the moor. So fierce was the rain that, long before we at last came down into Dufton, our wellington boots were literally overflowing and all three of us were soaked to the skin, our 'weatherproof' jackets proving to be no more useful than the dog's fur.

To complete a memorable day, when we reached the streets of Dufton, we discovered that the torrential rain had caused the storm drains and sewers to overflow, forcing us to splash through water up to two feet deep, trying not to look too hard at the objects carried past us on the flood.

Those who do not learn from their mistakes are doomed to repeat them. I set off from Appleby determined that this time, without fail, I would conquer High Cup Nick. The weather forecast was good, and, though the army were shooting on the ranges, I had planned a route that would take me high above the ranges, along the shoulder of the hills to Brough. What could possibly go wrong?

I walked over to Dufton from Appleby, a lovely walk through soft, undulating country, only slightly marred by the thuds, bangs and crashes from the ranges, and followed the Pennine Way up along the lip of High Cup Nick to the top. It was a spectacular sight, but I felt some sense of anticlimax at finally achieving my goal. I tracked on over the moor, ignoring the army's red danger signs, and passing the grouse shooting butts established by local people but now largely pirated by the army for their own private use, according to my poaching correspondent from Brough.

As I climbed back on to the ridge above Eden, the cloud dropped without warning, shrouding the fell, and cutting visibility to twenty yards.

'No problem to an old fell hand like me,' I thought, striding out purposefully through the mist. A few minutes later, my position on the ground did not seem to coincide with any feature marked on my map. 'No problem,' I thought. 'The wind is blowing up the face of the hills, I'll just walk into it until I drop below the cloud, get my bearings and then climb up again to rejoin my route.'

Apart from sliding out of control for fifty yards down a scree slope, I succeeded admirably, emerging amongst the old mines high on Hilton Beck. 'No problem,' I thought, consulting my map. 'All I have to do is keep to the track down to the point where a beck comes in from the east and then follow the beck right up to the ridge.' To this day, I am not sure whether, through tiredness or inattentiveness, I walked straight past the beck, or whether it does not actually exist; whichever it was, I eventually found myself still on the old mine track and only a mile or so from Hilton village.

'No problem,' I thought, once again. 'I'll just scramble over this hill and up the fell-side till I reach the ridge.' The shooting from the ranges had fallen silent some time before, and I was confident both that my navigation was now flawless and that, in any event, the army had declared a cessation of hostilities for the day. I breasted the hill, to find myself looking directly into an army observation tower perhaps half a mile away.

'That shouldn't be there,' I thought, standing tranfixed as the tanks on the ranges began firing again. There was a crash as a shell thudded into the hillside beneath me.

I am not a complete coward. I have faced a pub full of irate and thirsty farmers, five seconds after I have called 'Time', a dressing-room full of rugby league players five minutes after they have lost a Challenge Cup Final, and a living-room full of an angry father, five hours after curfew time for his daughter, and lived to tell the tale, but the closest I had previously come to being under fire was when jogging half a mile from Lord Whitelaw on a grouse shoot. Nothing in my suddenly very precious life had prepared me for the moment when I found myself looking down the gun-barrel of a tank. In fact it was a country mile away and its shells were exploding a safe distance below me, but this was scarcely a time for logic.

While my mind was still trying to come to terms with this new and fascinating experience, my legs were carrying me back over the hill and down to the track to Hilton at prodigious speed. When I finally stopped for breath, having put at least half a mile between me and my near-nemesis, I decided that I had taken ample exercise and had quite sufficient excitement for one day and turned my back on the hills around High Cup Nick, probably for ever.

I spent the evening in one of my favourite Appleby pubs, across the Sands, as the flat ground by the river is called, from the Eden. It is a pub with an excellent pint of beer, a blazing fire and a high-settled enclave where a congregation of 'doms' players were at their devotions, fumbling with their dominoes like the beads of a rosary.

Two farmers sat on stools at opposite ends of the bar, both staring blankly ahead of them. They favoured me with a brief glance and a curt nod, before resuming their scrutiny of the bar fittings. I bought a pint and stood at the bar, equidistant between them. As a rule I have a great liking for upland farmers. Without idealizing or sentimentalizing them unduly, they do seem to have a few less of the usual human failings and vices and rather more than the normal allotment of virtues too. There are at least two farmers who will be forever exceptions to that general rule, however: the ones I encountered propping up the bar that night.

About seventy pence worth of change already lay on the bar. 'Does this belong to one of them?' I asked the landlady, pointing towards the dominoes tables.

'No, a visitor left it there a few minutes ago. She may be back for it.' I left it lying there. The man to my right, an unusual figure of a farmer, fine-featured, quite slim and wearing a spotless blue boiler suit which even had neat creases in the trousers, swivelled to look at the coins, glanced at me and then resumed his contemplation of the bar.

I looked around the room, pausing to watch the dominoes for a minute, and when I turned back to the bar to pick up my pint, Blue Boiler Suit seemed to have moved along the bar a yard or so towards the small pile of loose change. I turned my back again, watching him out of the corner of my eye and saw him inching along the bar towards the money, like a caterpillar approaching a tasty leaf.

It took him a couple of minutes of stealthy advance, picking up his glass, drinking from it and then replacing it slightly further along the bar, before he reached his target. His arm came to rest on top of the change and, when he began his almost imperceptible journey back along the bar, the money had disappeared.

When he had reached the sanctuary of his corner, I turned and looked at the empty space on the bar. 'Oh look,' I said loudly, 'someone has taken the money from the bar. I was going to put it in the collection box for the little sisters of the poor, and now it's gone.' The farmer at the other end of the bar winked, the landlady gave me a puzzled smile and went back to polishing glasses, but Blue Boiler Suit sat tight, not turning to look at me, though the back of his neck went an impressive red, shading into purple. Five minutes later, he drank up and disappeared into the night.

'He'd have the pennies off a corpse's eyes would that one,' said the other farmer as the door closed. 'Good thing you kept your hand on your drink or he'd have supped that as well.'

'I thought all farmers were like that – Aberdonians without the generosity.'

We struck up a conversation and he showed himself unusually well-informed about world events. Most farmers regard the news as of only marginal importance to their lives, paying little attention to the problems of Nicaragua, Afghanistan or any other faraway places with strange-sounding names, coming alert only at the mention of farming, livestock or subsidies. Much more important is the common currency of rural life, gossip; zealously acquired, jealously hoarded, shrewdly traded.

Some find the gossip, the insistent curiosity, the half-heard remarks or the sudden silences when the subject enters a room, hard to take. Yet it is surely more natural for a community to talk about topics of which they have an intimate knowledge, than for a roomful of humourless Hampsteads to bemoan the appalling situation in El Salvador, or a winebarsworth of yuppies to argue whether South Koreans have more street cred than Taiwanese.

The farmer talked about his long-held desire to see more

of the world than the few acres of his farm, and I was enjoying his company almost as much as the warmth of the fire and the quality of the beer, when the conversation began to go rapidly downhill.

'What line of work are you in?'

'I'm a journalist,' I replied.

'Oh, you tell lies for a living then.'

'Something like that.'

'Well I'll tell you something you can put in your paper, they want to get all those scrounging buggers off the dole and make them work for a living like farmers have to. They should stop all these hand-outs to industries as well. That Maggie has only done half a job, she wants to get on and give the hard word to those buggers on the railways and in the mines. If they can't stand on their own two feet they should go under. No one featherbeds farmers, if we don't work, we starve.'

Every pub seems to have one, a pet bigot who occupies a corner and bores the pants off every passing customer with his tediously predictable opinions on an equally predictable range of issues; but this one was extremely well disguised: an urbane and reasonable manner to draw in the unwary victim, and then a blast of noxious opinions, delivered at close range, like a spray of slurry from his muckspreader.

I was going to switch to auto-pilot, smiling and nodding occasionally and making my escape as soon as I had finished my beer, but his last remark was too much to take.

'You farmers get more state hand-outs than anyone else,' I said. 'You make being on the dole look like an honourable occupation. You get subsidies for your stock, grants to plant things, grants not to plant things, grants to grub out hedges and trees, grants to plant them back again, payments to grow crops, payments for not growing crops, grants for buildings, grants for fencing, grants for walling. When you're not filling in claim forms for grants, you're poisoning the water with your silage run-off and your nitrate fertilizers, and disfiguring the landscape with your ugly buildings, for which, unlike mere mortals, you don't need planning permission. When you go to auction you get guaranteed prices for your stock and your crops as well, and even then you whinge about it all the way home in your brand-new Volvos. Your wives do twice the work that you do and don't belly-ache about it at all. If you lot tried standing on your own two feet, you'd fall over.'

I paused for breath, giving him the chance to try to reclaim the high ground.

'British farming leads the world. We're the most efficient industry in the country.'

'The most efficient at scewing money out of the government and the EEC. Bank robbers are just as efficient and they don't moan half as much as you lot do.'

He was beginning to remind me of the bigots I used to endure around the pubs of my home town of Bradford, who would rant about 'Pakis coming over here and taking our jobs', and then, half a minute later, without a trace of irony, complain, 'They're all on the dole, scrounging money instead of doing a decent day's work.'

He changed his tack. 'You'd all be running to us in wartime though, wouldn't you, you need us to keep the nation fed. And another thing, instead of complaining about our subsidies – and they're little enough I can tell you – what about complaining about all the money we send out to Africa and places like that. They want to let all those buggers in Ethiopia starve if they can't grow enough to feed themselves. They'll only breed again otherwise.'

I was genuinely shocked. Such views seemed even more obscene expressed in terms suggesting a logical and efficient solution to a difficult problem, than they would have done spat out by some crazed fanatic in a black shirt.

'I hope your sheep are barren, your hay crop rots and you fall off your tractor and break your miserable neck,' I said, leaving my pint on the bar and walking out before he had a chance to answer back. After being driven off the fells by a tank, to have let a farmer with fascist tendencies have the last word as well would have been too much dishonour for one day.

# ·Summer·

MIST clings to the fells in the early morning, waiting passively for the heat of the sun to disperse it. As the daylight strengthens, nesting golden plovers set up their eerie, monotone piping, till the fells seem full of the sound.

By the time the farmyards begin to stir, the mist has already been burned from the tops, though it still clings to the valley floor, grey tendrils following each beck and stream. Swallows sit chattering impatiently on the eaves of a barn by the Eden. High on the fells, lapwings are cartwheeling in the sunlight, while curlews soar above them, gliding back to earth uttering their haunting, mournful cry. Larks, almost invisible in the sky overhead, rain down a torrent of song. Sheep toil up the fell-sides towards the tops, away from the stinging hordes of insects below.

Before the mist has gone from the meadows, tractors are busy mowing the hay. The few meadows already cut and cleared, their stubble burned brown by the sun, await the rain that will bring the growth of new grass, the 'fog' as the farmers call it. Like the dead flowers and grasses and the husks of seed pods, the brown patches of cleared meadow signal that the year is already on the turn.

Gypsies at Fair Hill

June. I had spent a week wandering the fells between Eden and Swaledale, and after another day alone with the grouse, the curlew and the larks, I walked down to a village pub, as the evening shadows slipped down the fell-sides to the river.

I had been sitting on the terrace outside the pub for some time, drinking beer and watching the swallows skimming the surface of the river, when a good idea came to me; at least it seemed like a good idea at the time. 'I know,' I said to my boon companion on this long and liquid evening, 'I'm going to go over to Appleby for the Fair. I'll get up before dawn, drive over there and take some great photographs of Fair Hill, just as the dawn is breaking.'

The idea didn't seem quite so outstanding at 4 a.m., as I left the warm embrace of my bed for the cold shoulder of a damp night and followed the narrow, twisting road that crosses the bleak moorland separating Swaledale from the Eden Valley. For centuries, perhaps from as early as Roman times, miners scrabbled into this sour and sodden land, digging out lead from the dales and coal from the fell-tops, which was then carried by trains of pack-horses down to the smelting mills in the valleys below.

Miners would walk for an hour or more simply to reach the mine workings high on the fells, then, after a day's back-breaking labour in foul air and soaking wet conditions underground, they would face the same long walk back in their dripping clothes. In the grey light of a damp, false dawn, it was not hard to imagine the miners trudging over the green roads across the moor. Even on this June morning there was an edge to the wind keening across the moor; in winter it cuts like a knife.

From the lonely outpost of Tan Hill, the road crosses the moors for another five miles, passing no human habitation but the old toll gate house, dating from the late eighteenth century and unoccupied throughout the twentieth. At intervals the road is punctuated by snow poles – tall wooden poles that mark the line of the road for the snow ploughs and diggers that must often fight their way through a white anonymous winter land-scape, every feature shrouded in feet of snow.

Quartz-rich spoil from the heaps at the old lead mills, the cheapest and most easily accessible material, was used to surface this ancient road, causing it to sparkle in the morning sunshine. On this grey morning, however, there was only the mist, carrying the sounds of the sad piping of the golden plovers and the anxious calls of the sheep to their lambs.

As I reached the moor edge, the mist lifted for a moment, giving me a brief, familiar glimpse down into the valley below, a view stretching to the mountains of the Lake District and the shores of the Solway Firth, a lush prospect of rich farmland and vivid green grass. After crossing the dun-coloured moorland with its mosses and sour peat hags, fit only for heather and cotton grass, Eden looks perfectly named. To travellers from harsher, colder lands, it must really have seemed the promised land, flowing with milk, if not honey, the finest dairy land in England.

Dropping down from the fells towards the valley floor, the drystone walls gave way to hedges, with the road burrowing between high earth banks. I passed the gaunt knuckle of Brough Castle and reached Appleby, just as the grey and drizzly dawn was breaking.

The new Appleby bypass was driven straight along the old Roman road just below Fair Hill, once known as Gallows Hill, where travelling people have gathered for the Horse Fair for centuries. No doubt it was the best line for the road, though some might suspect darker motives; not everyone in Appleby loves the Fair. The travellers' caravans are a little more remote from town as a result, though not beyond the long arm of the law. I drove up towards the cluster of caravans, Romany wagons, flat-bed trucks and Transit vans that covered the site, huddled together as if for warmth against the cool of the night. As I pulled up, a police van at the corner of the site, parked, perhaps, in case this was another load of hippies on their way to another alternative Stonehenge, disgorged six policemen, eager for whatever diversion a dawn visitor like myself might offer.

'What are you doing here, son?' asked a sergeant a full twelve months older than myself. 'I'm going to take some photographs,' I explained, producing my tripod as Exhibit A for the defence. 'What for?' continued the sergeant, warming to his theme. 'For a book I'm writing.' I was tempted to add a few enquiries about whether I was violating a curfew or whether a state of emergency had been declared, but no one likes a smart-arse, least of all a bunch of grumpy policemen who need their sleep, so I left it there.

The sergeant was not to be shaken off the scent so easily, however. 'Why do you want to take pictures of a load of gypsies?' he enquired. 'Because they're interesting,' I replied innocently, unwittingly applying a blow-lamp to the fuse of temper that had been smouldering in the sergeant from the moment he was assigned to holding the frontier against these latter-day barbarian hordes.

'Interesting? What's interesting about a load of scruffy, dirty layabouts?' he demanded, immediately proceeding to answer his own question. 'Nothing. If you want to show something interesting, why don't you take pictures inside that barn over there?' Here his arm waved vaguely in the direction of Lancaster, some fifty miles away. 'Show all the filth they leave in there.' I said I'd consider it when I'd got a few shots of the caravans, and then left him to his rantings. I got the photographs I wanted, but I couldn't oblige him with the filth in the barn – I hadn't brought my flash-gun.

This free and frank exchange of views sums up the ambivalent relationship we have always had with gypsies. We have only to pass an old-fashioned Romany wagon on a country lane for our eyes to mist over, as we begin a monologue of the 'My God, that's the way to live, for two pins I'd give up the job at Bonkley's, let Tarquin's school fees and Fiona's riding lessons go hang and set off for a life on the open road' variety. The lure of the open road usually lasts as far as the next bend in it, however, and our admiration for the Romany way of life disappears as soon as a caravan comes to a halt near our town or village.

In the opinion of every self-appointed taproom expert up and down the country, gypsies – or travellers, to give them a less pejorative name – are dirty, devious thieves, rogues and villains who will steal the washing off your line and the gold fillings out of your teeth as soon as look at you. Appleby Fair is as good a place as any to find out the truth of this, for it attracts travellers from all over Britain.

Some Appleby residents share the opinions of the Fair Hill police contingent about this annual invasion of their sleepy little town, finding it rather like having Attila the Hun to stay on his summer holidays, but for others, particularly publicans and shopkeepers, Appleby Fair can be the time of a welcome, if temporary, Midas touch.

The Fair is claimed to be the largest of its kind in the world and dates from 1685, set up under the protection of a Charter from James II for the 'purchase and sale of all manner of goods, cattle, horses, mares, geldings'. The Charter refers to a Fair held in April, and 'Appleby New Fair' as it is known, dates from 1750, when the month was changed to June.

Fair Day itself is always the second Wednesday in June, exactly a week after that other great gypsy gathering, Derby Day at Epsom. Travellers begin arriving on the week-end before the Fair, and for a couple of weeks before that every byway, country lane and piece of common land for miles around seems to contain a caravan. An open-air church service is always held up on Fair Hill on the Sunday before Fair Day; on the night before the Fair there is more secular entertainment, harness racing, on Holme Farm Meadow.

The travellers also practise another, less official form of racing, done both for pride and for prodigious sums in bets, in which the participants race at dawn along a road, a dual carriageway or even a motorway, while a convoy of vans and cars blocks off the course to traffic at either end. The police know it goes on, but are usually powerless to intervene, for by the time they arrive on the scene, the race is over and the participants and spectators are heading for home, offering nothing more tangible than an air of injured innocence if stopped and questioned.

Despite the other attractions, the Fair is first and foremost a time when travellers indulge in their favourite sport of horse-trading, both with their fellows and with outsiders; these range from people looking for a pony for their children to the upland sheep farmers who have used the distinctive piebald ponies, 'Dales Galloways' as they call them, for centuries. Though tractors now do much of the farm work once carried out by horses, in winter snows that can stop a tractor in its tracks, a horse can still 'lead hay' through the drifts to fodder hungry sheep.

Having got my photographs and spent two cold hours waiting for the nearest transport café to open, I indulged in a massive and lengthy breakfast, before driving down into the centre of Appleby. I took up position on the bridge in the heart of the town and watched as a succession of travellers brought their horses down to the river to wash them in the broad, smooth-flowing Eden as it drifted through the town. While most of the horses are being preened to be sold, some horse owners are just doing it for 'flash' – showing off a fine horse, or themselves. I saw the same lad bring his horse down to the river three times, perhaps hoping to stir interest of a non-commercial kind among the girls watching from the bridge.

A good size crowd had gathered, some casting an eye over potential purchases, most just there for the show. Boys rode the horses bareback into the river in turn and then washed them down using a plastic bottle of washing-up liquid, a touch of new technology in an age-old ritual.

In the afternoon, the horse-trading began in earnest. A vast crowd thronged the Long Marton road, where the horses are run and spectators need swift reactions. One minute I was surrounded by people, the next there was a cry of 'Oi! Oi! Oi!' and the crowd parted to reveal a horse and rider bearing down like the wind. The effect was sufficiently shattering for me to break the UK all-comers' record for the standing jump, to the great amusement of the battle-hardened veterans around me, who swayed nonchalantly to one side, like roustabouts on a fairground ride, before resuming their conversation. I retired, red-faced, to calm my shattered nerves and salve my wounded pride, before returning to the fray.

Having torn through the crowd two or three times to advertise his wares, each vendor settled back to await offers from suitably impressed purchasers. It seemed appropriate to eavesdrop on the negotiations for the horse that had almost run me over, so I joined a small group gathered around the two principals, who were about to enter serious negotiations. The ensuing bartering was long and heated, with both participants egged on by the enthusiastic crowd, who derived as much pleasure from the wrangling over price as they had from watching the horses. Buyer and seller were subjected to a barrage of entirely unlooked-for advice as the spectators, like apprentice marriage guidance counsellors, tried to bring the two warring parties together.

To seal a deal all that was required was to spit and slap hands on a price, but both parties needed to satisfy their honour by walking away in disgust at least three times, and all the while the onlookers kept up their barrage of advice. 'Bid him another ten.' 'Away, it's all he's worth, shake hands.' 'That horse keeps his teeth in a jar by the bed, he's not worth half that price.'

Finally, as the sun sank lower in the sky, the two parties allowed themselves to be drawn together. With feigned reluctance and a small amount of aggrieved muttering, hands were slapped and the sale was made. No contract is needed and no cheques are accepted; a man's word is his bond and the only negotiable currency is cash. Even then the business is not quite complete, for the small matter of 'luck' must be attended to. 'Luck money' is paid on horse deals, as on virtually all livestock sales, but often the greatest good fortune attends the drinking companions, for the universal fate of luck money is to finish its life in some publican's till.

I watched the two participants step to one side to complete the deal; no paperwork is required, for I have yet to encounter a horse dealer who is registered for VAT. The buyer produced an enormous roll of ten pound notes, held together by a rubber band, from an inside pocket and counted off the agreed price. The seller licked his thumb and riffled through the notes at a velocity that reminded me of a farmer's description of an illiterate, but wealthy rival: 'He can't read or write, but by God, he can count.' The 'luck' was handed back, the two men shook hands, slapped each other on the back and the small knot of spectators drifted away, smiling to themselves; we all love a happy ending.

Both parties will normally commemorate the closing of the deal by retiring to the pub to celebrate their good fortune or drink away the memory of their folly, providing they can find a pub that is open. For some Appleby publicans, the Fair is a time to board up the windows and go into hiding, perhaps allowing the regulars in through a back door for a pint or two. Of the seven pubs in Appleby, five stay open but two are firmly shut. It is an attitude I have never understood, for those that welcome the travellers' money reckon that the bulging tills will be handsome compensation for any damage left behind when the travellers have moved on.

The publicans also have a fund of good stories for the long winter months to come. One told me of discovering a set of false teeth in the corner of the Gents, which he rinsed and put on the shelf. The next morning a traveller had staggered in, hung-over and toothless, having lost his false teeth in a mighty sneeze and been unable to find them in his drunken condition of the night before. When he seized on the proffered set, however, they would not fit. A similar accident had presumably befallen someone else, who had scooped up the wrong teeth and failed to notice the mistake. No one has ever returned the other set, so, unless it found use as a set of pastry crimpers, somewhere in Britain is a traveller who has not eaten a meal in comfort since the night he got drunk at Appleby Fair.

Even at the pubs that do open, they take the precaution of hiding their ornaments and taking up their carpets. That may be prudence or it may be merely pandering to old prejudices, but attitudes among a proportion of the people on both sides of the divide are so deeply entrenched that only surgery will remove them. For every virulent gypsy- or giorgio-hater there is another willing to live and let live, however, and there have been no serious threats to the future of the Fair since 1965, when complaints about nuisance and the near-blocking of the Long Marton road by travellers' vehicles led to an attempt to end the Fair for ever. A deputation of travellers argued successfully for its continuance then, and support for it, even among Appleby residents, remains far more widespread than the complainants would like to believe.

One Appleby native offered a welcome voice of sanity. 'We live such an idyllic life that the week-long Fair is a shock to the system, though nothing compared with the problems of city-dwellers. More and more such people are coming to Appleby to escape those problems, but they must accept the Fair as part and parcel of Appleby life before choosing to live here.'

As well as being a forum for horse-trading, Appleby provides one of the few chances for the travelling community to meet during the year, and much family business is settled there. Marriages may be arranged and disputes and old scores settled, often by the rough and ready justice of a bareknuckle fight. Fights between travellers and outsiders are not unknown, but even having added travellers to the already volatile mixture of young farmers, soldiers and liberal quantities of alcohol, trouble is surprisingly rare.

In the main, the travellers have come to meet old friends and enjoy themselves. What they would like is to be left alone

to get on with it, but the clash between two mutually uncom-
prehending cultures always makes that implausible. The
travellers need grazing for their horses. In the past the horses
would be turned out on to the roadside verges or the common
land, but both are in short supply in twentieth-century Britain
and the travellers will often take advantage of farmers' fields
instead.

Their dogs are expected to feed themselves and will be
turned out in the evening to bag whatever game they can find,
leading to more conflict with farmers and gamekeepers. Any
theft or disappearance in the area will also automatically be laid
at the travellers' doors, though many will have been carried out
by local 'hooks' using the presence of gypsies as a convenient
smokescreen.

It is hard to escape the feeling that the police and some of
the townsfolk would be happy to see Appleby Fair disappear
into history, and their actions and attitudes seem designed to
give that process a push. Police are drafted into Appleby in
vanloads like the one I encountered at dawn, and I saw them
stop and interrogate travellers as many as three or four times on
their way down into the town. Council workmen cut the
roadside verges the week before the Fair, removing the grazing
for the travellers' horses, while residents complain long and
hard about dirt, noise, theft and violence.

While some will moan about crime, however, others will
count their profits. The china shop in Appleby probably sells
more Crown Derby in one week than Bond Street manages in a
year, for the travellers have no great liking for banks or stocks
and shares. Good china is both a convenient means of storing
wealth and of displaying it to those privileged to be invited into
the caravan.

The old, horse-drawn Romany caravans have all but
disappeared now, and even the few still seen on Fair Hill have
often spent the year in mothballs, emerging blinking into the
early summer sunlight for the annual trek to Appleby. The true
status symbol among travellers is the motor-drawn caravan,
smothered in chrome, with etched, engraved and brilliant cut

windows, and, inside, the inevitable Crown Derby on display. It seems a bizarre contrast to an outsider: a life spent on mud-covered, scrap-infested wastelands, with no running water or sanitation – but inside the spotless caravans there is cut-glass and Crown Derby; 'all fur coat and no knickers', as they say in the North.

As well as the horse-drawn caravans, the old stand-bys of clothes-pegs, fortune-telling and knife sharpening have all but disappeared too. The staple trade of the modern traveller is in scrap metal, and there are countless non-Romany travellers – the Irish call them 'tinkers' – involved in it as well. There are still a few women telling fortunes on Fair Hill, however, and I joined a queue of giggling Appleby schoolgirls to discover what fate had in store for me. The crystal ball pronounced me a gentleman, though my Oxford tones may have helped the diagnosis, and I was promised fame and fortune. I warmed rapidly to both fortune-telling and my own fortune-teller in particular at this point, though fulfilling her later prediction that I would father two fine children may prove troublesome – I had a vasectomy ten years ago.

As the evening darkened, travellers began to gather around camp-fires and an occasional burst of a traditional gypsy song could be heard, though the predominant musical accompaniment was provided by the rather less traditional ghetto-blasters that most of the travellers' children seemed to be toting. I left the travellers to their pleasures and drove back towards Swaledale and sleep.

For all the often spurious charms of fortune-tellers and horse-traders, Appleby Fair remains a great event – earthy, noisy, dirty, and very much alive. The levels of crime and violence at the Fair are grossly exaggerated. There is more aggression in five minutes on a London commuter train than all day in Appleby, and the Fair is an event that puts the town firmly on the national map. Its fame brings thousands to Appleby every year, drawn by the Fair or by the associations of the name. Without it, Appleby might well become just another bypassed, obscure Cumbrian town, like its neighbour Brough, which could scarcely be accused of setting the pulses racing these days; most people stay on the A66 and pass by.

Some local residents delight in tales of the criminal outrages that take place around Appleby Fair, but my own straw poll of potential 'disgusteds of Acacia Crescent' suggested that those most opposed to the Fair were those who had retired to Appleby from elsewhere. The same dead hand of irreproachable geriatric gentility has bid fair to choke the life out of many small towns and villages in the northern rural retirement zones. This case above all is one for that wrinkled old hand to be given a savage crack across the knuckles.

Appleby Fair is the last of its kind in Britain. Long may it survive, however dirty, smelly and noisy it may be. Let the lace curtains twitch their exasperation for one week a year; for those seven days Appleby is alive, celebrating a tradition that goes back centuries and which provides a brief, bright splash of colour in the dun-coloured year of these Cumbrian fells.

# 11
# TEMPLE SOWERBY

Temple Sowerby

summer morning, pausing at the top of the bluff to the south-west and looking back over the roof-tops of the town, past Murton Pike, to the narrow, half-hidden valley of High Cup Nick. The river curved in a great arc below me, swollen into a flood by overnight rains, with branches, logs, even tree trunks swept along with it. On the far bank, the small alluvial plain enclosed by the river meander is the scene of a constant battle between river and farmer, the Eden carving away at the bank, the farmer dumping rock and rubble to hold it back.

Away to the north, I could see the prominent white shape of the 'golf ball' radar mast on Great Dun Fell. From this distance it looked more like a sinister, white toadstool. These radar stations on the Pennines mimic the Roman signalling posts that ran from York, by way of Stainmore, to Carlisle, each in line of sight of its neighbour to either side. Warnings of trouble from the Picts and Scots were quickly passed down the line, and reinforcements summoned. Eden's medieval inhabitants used church bells and bonfires to send similar warning of Scots raiders down the valley, but if the radar mast on Great Dun Fell ever sends warning of the perils it was designed to detect, its signal will presage a destruction more total than anything seen, even in Eden's battle-scarred history.

It was a signally depressing thought with which to blight a delightful morning. I let it go and walked on along a green way, past a hedgerow alive with birdsong. I picked my way through a track rutted by the wheels of a tractor biting deep into the soft, wet soil and passed the by now familiar mound of black-bagged 'big bales'.

As if in warning that, even in high summer, winter is never far away in these northern hills, the sky darkened and a squall of icy wind hit me in the face, rain stinging my cheeks; then, just as quickly, it was gone. I passed a hedgerow grubbed out of a field, the remnants piled in four sacrificial pyres, and blundered into the day's first quagmire, applying an Eden mud pack to the front of my trouser legs. Cold, muddy water seeped slowly down into my wellington boots.

At Bolton Bridge I came back to the river, which was stained the colour of the Eden rock, with every obstruction to its headlong flow, like the tree branches drooping into the water, festooned with river debris. I leaned on the parapet of the bridge for a while, watching wood and debris swept along by the swollen Eden. A river is a massive transporter of material, slicing to and fro across the face of the land like a cutting machine at the coal face and dropping the excavated material into the water, which, like a colliery conveyor belt, carries it relentlessly away.

I crossed to the far bank, rewarded by a sight that would have had Ian Fleming snapping his cigarette holder in excitement: the twin phalluses of two enormous concrete farm silos, framed by the thrusting conical peaks of Dufton and Knock Pikes. Could their peaks be hard with passion, or was it only granite?

I emerged on to the main road at Kirkby Thore, a village dominated by the gypsum plant that provides virtually all of the local employment. It was a mercifully brief chance to savour the delights of diesel fumes, and I quickly escaped on to a footpath heading back to the Eden. As I walked towards the river, ahead was the first sight of the Lake District mountains, with Blencathra's saddleback dominating the skyline.

Here the Pennines begin to curve away to the north, but the river continues westward for a few miles before turning to follow, carving a course through the soft alluvial lands in an ever broadening valley. A line of trees, once marking the bank, are now stranded by the river, which cuts away at the exposed bank behind them, leaving them Canute-like, waist-deep in water. Once more there were the signs of a farmer's attempts to hold back the river by dumping rock and rubble, but the Eden can only be delayed, not defeated, for its patience is limitless. A farmer may spend fifty years fighting it, but one flood, one night, will defeat his struggle. The bank will have changed beyond recognition, with nothing more than a string of fence posts dangling from their barbed wire in the water to show where he had tried to hold the line.

A pair of oyster-catchers flew away from me downstream, peeping indignantly at the disturbance, as I again turned away from the river, walking up towards Temple Sowerby. I looked back from the top of a small hill, to see the Eden curving away through beautiful woodland, the sunlight dappling the water.

When I reached the village, a mark on the wall of the church informed me that I was now 348 feet above sea level. Inside, a bizarre table of kindred and affinity supplied the equally useless information that a man may not marry his: 'mother, daughter, father's mother, mother's mother, son's daughter, daughter's daughter, sister, father's daughter, mother's daughter, wife's mother, wife's daughter, father's wife, son's wife, father's father's wife, mother's father's wife, wife's father's mother, wife's mother's mother, wife's son's daughter, wife's daughter's daughter, son's son's wife, daughter's son's wife, father's sister, mother's sister, brother's daughter, sister's daughter' – and vice versa. I had an uneasy feeling that most of these were probably one and the same person, but could not summon the enthusiasm to disentangle the relationships to make sure.

No doubt the prohibitions on incest and marriage between close blood relatives had to be strictly enforced when communities were very isolated from each other and the pool of available marriage partners was small. The consequences of in-breeding are still apparent in some of the more remote upland villages, where virtually everybody is at least a cousin of everybody else and the number of genetic defects is far higher than would be expected from the size of the population.

My own major genetic defect, on the other hand, seems to

be an inability to time my arrival at the end of a walk before closing time. I headed purposefully for the pub, a village local shading over strongly into a roadhouse, with a fair smattering of Sierras and Cavaliers in the car park. I have to admit I scarcely cut a sartorial dash, wearing wellingtons and my oldest jeans, both liberally encrusted with mud, but after all, this is a rural area.

I entered the pub and spotted the landlord, who looked the type to call his customers 'squire' and whose idea of informality was probably a check shirt and cravat. I eyed the carpet in the lounge bar uneasily, decided against it, and enquired:

'Do you have more of a scruff's bar, a taproom, that I could use? I don't want to dirty your best carpet.'

He looked me up and down with ill-disguised contempt. 'I most certainly do not.'

'Never mind,' I said, gritting my teeth and reminding myself that this was the only pub for four miles, 'I'll sit out here in the hall. Could I get some lunch and a pint of bitter please?'

'We've finished doing lunch, and anyway I'm just closing,' he said, stalking off back into the lounge. I could distinctly hear the sounds of glasses being re-filled as I contemplated my next move, but I resigned myself to a chocolate bar and a soft drink from the village shop instead, and left.

'The way things are going it will be half-day closing at the shop,' I told myself, as I crossed the road. It was. I walked back towards Appleby alongside the main road, my stomach grumbling. The grass verge was both a shocking indictment of carborne litter louts and a reminder of the multitudes of different junk foods I could have been consuming. Almost every step of the way, there was a drinks can, a plastic bottle, a cigarette packet or a sweet wrapper. There was even a polystyrene fast-food container, though the nearest MacDonalds must have been at least twenty miles away. It served as a timely reminder that walking through Eden is only half the story, for while I was watching the river transporting its burden of soil, wood and rock down to the sea, a convoy of trippers and travellers was dumping almost as much waste material along the roadside back towards its source.

I had resigned myself to walking all the way to Appleby before I could eat, but I chanced on a transport café and bolted down a couple of slices of toast, trying not to notice the all-pervasive smell of damp and the silver trails left by the slugs' nocturnal excursions over the carpet, which the owners either had not noticed or had ceased to care about.

I collected my car from Appleby, and as this was to be my last day within the realm of Lady Anne, I decided to visit another of the stone monuments which increasingly seemed to punctuate my journey through Eden: the Countess Pillar, a short distance from Brougham Castle. It had marked a water-shed in her life, perhaps it might also mark one in my travels – maybe tomorrow I would reach a pub before closing time.

The Countess Pillar stands just to the side of the road, erected in 1656 to commemorate Lady Anne's last parting from her mother, forty years before. They rode out together from Brougham Castle, then parted at the brow of this small hill, her mother riding on towards London, as Lady Anne turned back to the castle, never to see her again.

The Pillar has sundials on three faces; on the other, two carved and painted shields, a skull and the misleading date 1654. The inscription describes her parting from her 'good and pious mother . . . in memory whereof she also left an annuity of £4 to be distributed to the poor within this parish of Brougham every second day of April forever, upon the stone table hard by'. The stone table still stands there and the money is still distributed, Lady Anne's last link to her people.

I turned back towards Temple Sowerby, resolving to reward myself for the day's hardships with an overnight stop at an expensive hotel and restaurant there. The surroundings were excellent, and if the cuisine did not quite match the owners' admittedly very high aspirations, I was too hungry and tired to care. I had thought of returning to the pub, imma-culately dressed, to spend half an hour being patronizing to mine slightly-less-than-genial host, but it seemed scarcely worth the effort for so petty a motive, and I remained in the hotel restaurant instead, demolishing a bottle of potent Australian red wine.

There were six other diners, four of them men eating alone. We all sat at separate tables, pretending to read our books and straining to catch the muted conversation of a couple who had the unmistakable look of two work colleagues preparing for a brief bout of marital infidelity.

I whiled away a happy hour, eavesdropping on them as they ate their dinner and, by the time I had finished my bottle of wine, the idea of returning to the pub had, unsurprisingly, become much more appealing. I strolled across the road and into the pub, discovering that there actually is a scruff's bar – or that would be my description anyway; the landlord probably calls it 'the smoking room'. Propping up the bar was a small, white-haired old man, who had faced and triumphed over one of the most difficult decisions which trouble men in their declining years: whether to wear the waistband above or below the paunch.

Modernists insist that the beer gut should jut, or more often sag, proudly out above the trousers, straining the shirt buttons, while a stout leather belt, often buried by rolls of flesh, performs a detour underneath, allowing the trousers to retain a precarious hold on the hips. My man in the pub was clearly a member of the old school, however. His suit trousers completely covered his paunch, the waistband almost on a level with his nipples. The trousers were held up by the shortest length of exposed braces that I would have believed possible. Normally the waistcoat of his ageing blue suit would have kept the engineering arrangements discreetly concealed, but it flapped open inside his jacket, exposing the braces to my fascinated stare.

We chatted as we drank and he told me some local lore and legend, including a story of the annual Liars Competition, which used to be held every May Day on the village green.

'The first prize was awarded to the biggest liar on the day. Well, the Bishop of Carlisle was passing by and he stopped to see what all the crowd and commotion was about. He started giving them a sermon on the evils of lying, saying, "I never told a lie in my life." Well that was it, they stopped the contest and awarded him the prize,' he said, creasing with laughter.

He had been looking meaningfully at his empty glass for a minute or two, so I bought him a beer.

'Was that story true, or was that a lie as well?'

'It's as true as I'm standing here,' he said, sitting down again on a bar stool.

# 12
# LONG MEG
# AND
# LACY'S CAVES

Long Meg & Her Daughters

THE NEXT MORNING, FEARING
further problems in obtaining lunch, I took the precaution of
eating a gargantuan breakfast. This included porridge with
Cointreau and fresh orange, a hideous – but deliciously
decadent – perversion of the Scots' parsimonious breakfast
traditions that would undoubtedly have caused Robert de Brus
to lay waste the whole of Eden in reprisal.

Stomach bulging, I walked out of Temple Sowerby along
Tannery Lane, past a long, ruinous barn and an equally
decrepit dovecote: the remains of the Tannery. Even in their
present sad state, the buildings have the sort of charm and
character that would have an estate agent thumbing excitedly
through his thesaurus for fresh superlatives. It is hard to
imagine such fine prospective bijou residences being allowed
to crumble away anywhere else in England, but that is part of
Eden's charm.

I walked up the lane and across the fields to an even more
bijou residence, Acorn Bank, a fine four-storey manor house
with a stunning view out over Eden. Now a Sue Ryder Home,
it was once the local base of the Knights Templar. They were
valiant fighters in the Crusades and grew to be a rich and
powerful organization, with Temples throughout Europe.
Although their secrecy and mysterious rituals did not endear
them to outsiders, any more than Freemasonry does today, it
was their burgeoning wealth and influence that caused their
downfall. They were accused of crimes that dared not speak
their name, including sodomy and quite possibly rum and the
lash as well. The fact that the accusations were false scarcely
mattered; confessions were extracted, heads were removed
and assets seized.

'Their great wealth and power rendered them insolent and formidable,' wrote Pennant, another of the band of eighteenth-century tourists. 'Under pretence of crimes of the most horrid nature, their persons were seized, their riches confiscated and their order totally suppressed in 1332.' It was a highly profitable exercise for the English Crown and one that was to be repeated two hundred years later by Henry VIII, whose Dissolution of the Monasteries proved to be even more rewarding. The Knights Hospitallers, who had succeeded to the Knights Temple in Sowerby, found themselves dispossessed in their turn, lending some irony to the name of the herb, Good King Henry, which is one of many ancient herbs growing in Acorn Bank's famous herb garden.

I walked down the drive away from Acorn Bank, past some of the oaks that gave the house its name, for they are such fine specimens that the acorns were regularly collected for tree nurseries. At the end of the drive is another fine specimen, a sequoia, the giant Californian redwood, planted soon after the tree's first introduction from the New World.

I followed the country lanes that led me past a beck like the infant Eden and then up a steep hill, with Stamper's sprawling agro-industrial complex to either side, a smart modern bungalow in its grounds. This is another facet of life in Eden which seems unique to rural areas. When a businessman makes it big in London, the last thing he would wish to do is build a house inside his factory gates. He heads for leafy suburbia and commutes to work. In Eden, on the other hand, it is by no means uncommon to see factories, builders' merchants, car showrooms and all kinds of other businesses with the owners' living accommodation built right alongside. The dislocation between work and home which has increased everywhere else since the nineteenth century does not seem to have taken root quite so strongly here. People do not see anything necessarily ugly about the place that provides their living, and the idea of spending twenty minutes, never mind an hour or two, travelling to work strikes them as absolutely ridiculous. I have a feeling that they may be right.

At the top of the hill, the main street of the village of Culgaith frames Great Dun Fell. On this cloudless, hot summer morning, it looked as if I could walk straight up the main street and on to the summit. Appearances can be deceptive, and instead I turned off to follow a footpath running straight through the garden of a bungalow. I hopped over a stile next to the greenhouse, passed the inevitable mound of black bags, hurdled a gate and landed squarely in the middle of the first morass of the day. When I raised my eyes from my mud-stained wellingtons, to the east was a stunning view of the whole Cross Fell range.

For the first time there were no intervening pikes or hills, just the gently sloping valley floor and then the Pennines rising up to the heights of Great Dun Fell and Cross Fell, the highest summits on the whole Pennine range. To the west, across the broad expanse of Eden, were the mountains of the Lake District.

Once more, without me being aware of the transition, the landscape had changed character. I was walking through gently undulating grassland, following lanes winding away into clumps of trees. There were long perspectives and far vistas. I walked a mile without seeing a single human being.

It was a morning so clear and bright that, had I been on top of Cross Fell instead of looking up at it, I might have had the chance of the fabled sight of both Irish and North seas from the summit. That would wait for another day, another time, however, for I was enjoying striding out on these long, lonely tracks.

A pair of kestrels burst out of the woods ahead of me, giving a twittering cry, and in a corner of the wood I passed a grizzled-looking man, perhaps younger than his lined face and white, three-day growth of stubble suggested. He was standing outside a ramshackle construction, like a squashed wooden horse-box. It had an ill-fitting door and a bit of a chimney poked out through the roof. His dog, a lurcher, had given tongue as I approached, and the man was pulling a flannel shirt over his head as I reached him.

'You walking through?' he asked.

'Yes, over to Lazonby. Do you live here?'

'Hereabouts.'

I asked him a few more questions, but his replies became even more monosyllabic and it was clear that he was anxious to be left alone in his woodland kingdom, monarch of all he surveyed. I could sympathize with his feelings, for at my Pennine pub I used to enjoy nothing better than climbing to the top of the hill and surveying 'my' territory, alone at the centre of fifty square miles of moorland with no other human being to dispute my sovereignty. The illusion was punctured as soon as the first bobbing back-pack of the day's first hiker appeared over the horizon, and I used to resent them, as I'm sure this old man of the woods resented me.

I left him and his dog to undisputed possession of their territory and walked on, enjoying the long tree-lined vistas flanking the track ahead. The drystone walls to either side of the track, once so painstakingly built, had outlived their purpose and were crumbling and collapsing. Two herons flapped lazily away at my approach. There was no habitation in sight, for the few farmhouses in the area were all tucked away behind low ridges.

I had three objectives in mind for the day's walking. The ultimate one was to reach Lazonby; the penultimate was to see Long Meg and her Daughters, a megalithic stone circle, second in size only to Stonehenge; and the other, despite the massive intake of porridge with Cointreau, was to reward myself for getting up so early and walking so far and so vigorously with a stop for lunch at the pub at Little Salkeld, near Long Meg. I knew there was a pub, because my eagle eye had detected the vital PH symbol on the Ordnance Survey map. After my twin problems of mud and closing time on the previous day, I was doing my best to avoid both. I was in ample time for lunchtime pub opening, but avoiding mud was invariably difficult, and often impossible.

I had now left the open country and rough woodland behind, and was back among the typical Eden pastures, meadows and small villages. The views of the Pennines and the mountains of the Lake District were stunning, but the conditions underfoot were less delightful. Between the neighbouring villages of Winskill and Hunsonby I encountered some ground that the Irish racing fraternity would describe as 'yielding'; the English would simply and more accurately call it 'bottomless'. Having sloshed and squelched my way up into the village, I took a lane beside a barn wall grooved dramatically by wind and rain and was immediately faced with another stretch of heavy going. The lane had been so trampled, manured and mired by cattle, over so many years, that, had the mud been bottled, it would have made the Sahara bloom in twenty minutes flat. There is an old saying that the farmer's foot is the best manure; there must have been an awful lot of farmers treading this lane.

I glared balefully at the nearest herd of cows, holding them personally responsible for the state of the lane. They stared unemotionally back at me, neither confirming nor denying the rumour. I battled on and eventually reached the promised land, a stretch of green lane that actually justified the adjective, its predecessors having been nothing but brown, stinking mud.

For the first time in a while, I could raise my eyes from the ends of my boots, to discover that Eden had once more narrowed to an obvious valley as it swung to the north. A low range of hills rose up from the far bank of the river, which flowed unseen a mile or so to the west, while the wall of the Pennines still rose to the east. My green lane wound pleasantly between the hedgerows, dropping down to a little beck. I paused and scrupulously washed the mud from my wellington boots, before carrying on up to Little Salkeld for a pint and a bite to eat in what I had decided would be a delightful village inn. The picture had already formed in my mind: lime-washed walls, a thatch, perhaps even roses and honeysuckle twining around the door, a pint of good local beer, cool from the stone cellar, a chunk of rough brown bread, a lump of tangy cheese, and a wooden bench outside the door, where I could sit watching the swallows' flight and listening to the birdsong.

Even another patch of clinging mud on my way up to the village didn't spoil my mood, as I cleaned my boots on the grass by the side of the lane and walked up the hill to the pub, the Druid's Head. It looked delightful, set back from the road, with a low wall enclosing a small garden. There was only one problem: it was no longer a pub, having been sold and converted into private houses. Cruel fate. I strangled a sob and walked on up the hill, a lump in my throat and nothing in my stomach, beerless and lunchless once more.

This was not perhaps the best state of mind or body to approach an ancient monument, but my grumbling mind and rumbling stomach were silenced by my first sight of Long Meg and her Daughters, stone witnesses of almost the whole of man's history in Eden. Unlike many other stone circles, they survived the anti-pagan fervour of eighteenth-century religious zealots almost unaltered from the condition described by Reginald Bainbrigg in the sixteenth century. 'Besides Little Salkeld . . . wher the Romaines have fought some great battle, ther standes certaine . . . pyramides of stone, placed ther in the manner of a crown. They are commonlie called meg with hir daughters. They are huge great stones, long meg standes above the ground in sight XV fote long and tre fathome about.'

Long Meg is mother not only to her stone daughters, who number about seventy – I lost count while walking the perimeter of the oval – but also to several legends. The survival of the stones owes much to these legends and also to one act of atmospheric, if not divine, intervention. It is claimed that the original Long Meg was either a virago or a witch, though medieval men may not have seen any great need for a distinction between the two. She held orgies on the sabbath with her lovers and daughters, for which mortal sin they were all turned to stone.

It was believed that if a piece was broken off the stones it would bleed, and that if you could circle the stones twice, counting them, and come up with the same number both times, either the stones would come back to life or the devil

would appear. That last legend caused a brief frisson when I
came across it while researching in a library, although the fact
that I managed to lose count altogether on the first circuit
suggested that I was not in too much risk either of eternal
damnation, or, disappointingly, of a sabbath orgy either.

In 1725 Colonel Lacy of Salkeld Hall decided to prove the
power of modern, Christian man over ancient, pagan superstition, by having the stones destroyed. His workmen were
ordered to blow up some with gunpowder and cut up the rest to
make milestones, but as they started the work, such a ferocious
storm broke out that they fled in terror from the thunder and
the lightning bolts. From then on, Long Meg and her
Daughters were allowed to stand undisturbed. After suffering a
similar storm on one of my fruitless assaults on High Cup Nick,
I was wholly in sympathy with the decision.

Wordsworth's first sight of Long Meg stirred him to his
usual careworn raptures:

> A weight of awe, not easy to be borne
> Fell suddenly upon my spirit – cast
> From the dread bosom of the unknown past,
> When first I saw that family forlorn.

The massive, rough-hewn stones form an ellipse perhaps
one hundred yards across, with Long Meg standing aloof on her
own. She is fifteen feet tall and her four corners face the four
points of the compass. The setting midwinter sun aligns with
her across the exact centre of the circle. The site it commands is
as impressive as the monument itself, for from here almost the
whole of Eden can be encompassed, with uninterrupted views
to the Lake District, the Howgills and the great sweep of the
Pennines right back to the hills flanking the source of Eden,
Hugh Seat and Wild Boar Fell.

I leaned my back against Long Meg, hoping she would
forgive the familiarity, and let my eyes roam over the length
and breadth of Eden. From this perspective, its communities,
apparently so insular and isolated, were all revealed as subjects
of the river. Whether they stood on its banks, or out of sight of

the river at the foot of the hills, the land they farmed, the livestock they grazed, were by its gift. Neither man, nor soil, nor trees, nor rocks, nor the hills themselves could stand against it.

Water and air, the softest, least substantive elements in Eden, can tear away the soil, overthrow trees and boulders, force whole hillsides to move, and break the will of men. By its very presence in those closed communities, the river flowing endlessly through tells of different places, broader horizons. It carries off earth, wood and rocks, and draws away the young life, the salmon in the river, the birds from the fells, even the children of farmers, made restless, like me, by the mere sight of Eden, drawn to follow to its end, to see the world beyond its walls. Yet if it takes away, Eden also gives back: silt spread on the water meadows, salmon returning to spawn, birds to nest, people to the land where they were born, even Eden water given back as rain to the fells by the clouds streaming in from the sea.

It was to be my last all-encompassing view of Eden. The wall of the Pennines would from now on shield the upper valley from me as I walked close to the river bank, following it beneath the canopy of the trees. There could be no more stunning remembrance of the whole of Eden than that which I took away with me as I started back down the hill towards Salkeld and the river.

A few yards along the lane leading away from Long Meg, a farmer's hand-lettered sign, nailed to a tree, warned: 'DANGER. Please leave no litter, dangerous to cattle.' Fifty yards away, at the side of the lane, was an empty plastic fertilizer bag, abandoned by a farmer.

At the bottom of the hill, having passed Little Salkeld's former public house with another reproachful look, I came back within sight of the Eden, which had grown appreciably since I left it at Temple Sowerby, fed by one of its largest tributaries, the Eamont. Across the river is Great Salkeld, the two villages separated since a great flood swept the bridge away in the fourteenth century.

Here the river and railway are re-united as the Settle–Carlisle crosses the Eden for the last time, continuing to run close by on the far bank for several more miles, before curving away into Carlisle as the Eden sweeps round in a great arc to the north. As the railway swept across the Eden on a graceful, seven-arched viaduct, I followed the long disused sidings to the old Long Meg gypsum mine on the east side of the river.

Ahead the Eden disappeared into a gorge, cascading over 'Boiling Force Weir', where once there was an ancient bridge, guarded by a small castle. Force Mill still stands on the far bank, and a few massive chunks of masonry still lie at either side of the river, hinting at the considerable size of the weir.

As I passed the ruinous remains of the mine buildings, I startled two deer, which bounded away through the woods ahead of me, their white rears bouncing out of view. The path wound through dense woodland, emerging by a sandy beach on a bend of the river. I paused to watch the water drifting through this idyllic landscape and, looking up, I saw the arched entrances of Lacy's Caves in the red sandstone cliff face ahead of me. When not attempting to blow up Long Meg, Colonel Lacy had busied himself planting the woodland through which I had been walking, and he had also had these strange-looking caves carved out of the soft Eden rock.

The path to the caves is cut through a shoulder of rock, with the cave entrances twenty feet or so above the Eden, which flows by at the foot of the cliff. A series of inter-connecting arched caves are carved from sandstone so soft that when I drew my fingers across it, they came away powdered with grains of rock.

I have seen it suggested that these caves were intended for use as wine cellars, but that seems implausible, not least because, with the hall a mile or so away, it would have been one hell of a long way to send the butler for another bottle, if they ran out during a dinner party. There was a great fashion in the eighteenth century for romantic caves and ruins, and Colonel Lacy surely had them created for that reason. He even employed a hermit to live in them, another popular rich man's fad at the time, which made it even less likely that he would have risked having a very happy hermit and no wine at all.

The caves provide a lovely view out over the Eden, and I sat down on a bench at the back of the first cave, to enjoy the view in the afternoon sunlight streaming through the trees. I was so rapt in contemplation that I failed to hear the approach of a young couple and was subjected to an abrupt *pensus interruptus* by their sudden appearance, the man intoning a speculation on the caves' origins from his guidebook. I listened long enough to save myself some research time later and then, arcadia no longer mine alone, I abandoned the caves and returned to the path along a delightful stretch of river; delightful in appearance, that is, for the innocent path held a couple of pitfalls for the unwary.

After the turbulence of Force Mill and the gorge past Lacy's Caves, the river had resumed a more sedate progress, drifting between thickly wooded banks. As the path climbed the side of a hill, I found myself in a morass made barely passable by the branches scattered in the swamp. I fought my way through, sweating and cursing, heaved a sigh of relief and climbed over a stile into an apparently innocuous field. I instantly sank into a bog that lapped a sixteenth of an inch from the top of my wellington boots.

I had whinged periodically about mud, bogs and swamps all the way through Eden, but now I unreservedly withdrew all previous allegations. Those that came before were unfit to even kiss the hem of this morass, it was truly a world championship contender. Boy scouts would sink into it up to their woggles, frogs would spurn it, even flies alighting on its surface would be swallowed by it. The route of the footpath lay five yards away, lower down the field, but it might as well have been five miles. I looked up the field instead, and thought I could detect a marginal improvement in the going underfoot. I had formed a strong attachment to my wellingtons by this point – we had, literally, been through a lot together – but I faced a major problem in retaining contact with them. They would enter the swamp willingly enough at each step, but were strangely reluctant to rise from it, perhaps regarding it as the wellington equivalent of a warm steaming bath on a cold winter day.

The only way to make any progress without leaving my footwear behind was to grip the top of one wellington with both hands and half-lift and half-drag my foot out of the mud, lowering it reluctantly back in a few inches closer to my goal, and then changing hands to the other boot. It must have looked like Quasimodo, trying to walk upright while simultaneously carrying a vat of boiling lead at knee level; it felt like it too. After ten minutes of painful progress, in which I only lost contact with a wellington twice, forcing me to stand like a heron on one leg, while digging elbow-deep in the morass for the missing boot, I emerged not far from exhausted and covered in mud.

I wiped off the worst encrustations and then followed the path on for another few hundred yards, emerging on to a road, where I met a fresh-faced, pink-cheeked hiker, clad from head to toe in approved hiking gear and heading in the direction from which I had just come. He reminded me of a particularly unctuous boy scout leader, and I formed an instant and entirely unreasonable dislike for him.

'How's the track further on?' he enquired with a pleasant smile.

'Absolutely no problem at all, really good walking,' I replied, with a certain economy in my use of the truth. I could see him eyeing my mud-splattered clothes and wellingtons, and a flicker of suspicion momentarily darkened his cheerful countenance, but I swiftly set his mind at rest.

'I've been exploring the old mines,' I lied, 'that's why I'm all muddy.'

I left him with a cheery wave as he marched on, unsuspecting, towards his doom. 'No matter what your troubles, there is always someone worse off than yourself,' as my old grandfather used to say. On this occasion I had made absolutely sure of it, and I wandered on with a lighter step and a malicious sense of glee, my only regret being that I would be too far out of range to hear the screams as his shiny new hiking gear got its slimy christening.

I could see journey's end for the day, Eden Bridge at Lazonby, across the fields ahead, and I let out a whoop of delight, causing panic to a family of moorhen on the river, which scattered in all directions, diving for cover beneath the overhanging canopy of flood debris.

Eden Bridge is one of the earliest on the Eden and one of the finest, with four irregular arches, each a different size, over the river itself, and another two on the near bank to allow flood water to pass. I crossed the bridge, using one of its recesses, originally built as refuges from livestock or wagons, to sidestep a lorry filling the bridge.

While waiting for the traffic to clear, I decided that in order to avoid another mudbath on the next stage of the journey, I should propitiate the Eden with an offering. I was earning some money from the river, so it seemed only right, in the local tradition, for me to let it have a bit of luck money back. I tossed a luck penny into the river from the bridge, then decided that a penny was probably insufficient in these inflationary times and threw in a luck shilling, five pence, as well.

After a five-hour walk, for the second day running I arrived at my destination just as the pubs were closing. I called at the local shop, miraculously open, fell upon a pie and asked if there was anyone in the village who might want to earn a few quid driving me back to Temple Sowerby. 'Hang on a minute and I'll go and ask,' said the friendly assistant, disappearing through the back door. A minute later a male head insinuated itself around the door, gave me an appraising look and retracted itself. Shortly afterwards, the assistant reappeared. 'I'm sorry, there doesn't seem to be anyone around.' Normally the offer of a tax-free 'foreigner' would have had one or two takers, but perhaps I looked like a snooper from the DHSS or the Inland Revenue on a walking tour of some of the muddier parts of the North, or perhaps, understandably, they just didn't want their car upholstery soiled. I abandoned the attempt and telephoned for a taxi from Penrith.

It arrived inside fifteen minutes, fast going for eight country miles, and its driver chain-smoked all the way to Temple Sowerby, regaling me with tales of the scandalous extortion visited by his peers in Blackpool on the annual Penrith taxi drivers' outing.

'Thirty-two of us made the same journey in eight taxis and no two of them had the same reading on the meter. It's a bloody disgrace.'

'But your meter's not even switched on,' I pointed out, helpfully.

'No, it's a standard charge for this journey.'

'You get a lot of people travelling by taxi from Lazonby to Temple Sowerby, then, do you?'

'No, I think you're the first one,' he replied, deadpan. I still got change from ten pounds for a twenty-mile round trip, no doubt extortionate in Eden, but for someone who had been in a London taxi less than a week before, it seemed almost a crime to pay so little.

# ·ᴀutumn·

'IN these mountains is a very remarkable phenomenon . . . . it is called a HELM-WIND. A rolling cloud, sometimes for three or four days together, hovers over the mountain tops, the sky being clear in other parts. When this cloud appears, the country people say the helm is up; which is an Anglo-Saxon word, signifying properly a covering for the head, from whence comes the diminutive helmet. This helm is not dispersed or blown away by the wind, but continues in its station, although a violent roaring hurricane comes tumbling down the mountain, ready to tear up all before it. Then on a sudden ensues a profound calm. And then again alternately, the tempest, which seldom extends into the country above a mile or two from the bottom of the mountain.'

Nicolson and Burn

*History and Antiquities of Westmorland and Cumberland*

# 13
# CROSS FELL AND THE FELL-SIDES

The Fountain at Dufton

who had flocked to Eden in the spring, and crowded the villages throughout the summer, gathered for the last time before their autumn migration, lining the lanes like the swallows on the telephone wires, then disappeared just as abruptly, leaving only a handful of stragglers behind.

I had waited for the last deck-chair to be furled, the last caravan to wobble its interminable way down the narrow lanes, the last coach party to drop the last ice-cream wrapper, the last hiker to disappear over the hill. The children were back at school, the Ladas, Skodas and Yugos safely back in their garages until the following Easter, and Eden was once more at peace. It seemed safe to emerge from my summer quarters and take up my journey through Eden again.

I had left home on a cold, clear autumn morning, but when I came in sight of Cross Fell, the Helm was up. The summit was capped in cloud and an icy wind was howling down the fell-sides. I had the choice of carrying on with my planned walk anyway, despite the certainty of frozen extremities and an ache in my east-bound ear, or spending the day inside the warm cocoon of the car, driving through the fell-sides instead. 'It takes more than a breath of wind to put me off a walk,' I muttered to myself, consulting the road map.

Half an hour later, I was deep in the fell-sides, driving through a succession of villages with houses huddled together round the green like wagon trains about to be attacked by Indians. That arrangement was equally valuable in restricting the ravages of the Helm wind and the Scots. Access to the villages was by narrow gaps between the houses, like the

Wiends in Appleby, which could be easily barricaded and defended against raiders. If there was no time to drive the stock up into the hills, to be hidden there until the danger was past, it was herded on to the village green, within the protective laager of the houses. Long after the Scots raiding had ceased, the narrow 'gates' into the village continued to be walled up as protection from the Helm wind and the winter weather; in Milburn this was still being done in 1826.

In tribute to the ferocity of the Helm wind, the village houses turn their backs to Cross Fell, with scarcely a north- or east-facing window to be seen. The Helm can blow at any time of the year, but it is most common in autumn and early spring. It is caused by the meeting of air streams from the east and west coasts. When the cold easterlies meet the warmer westerlies, the cold air is forced down the slopes of the fell-side, its velocity increased by the shape of Cross Fell. A bank of cloud, the Helm Cap, sits motionless on the summits, extending from Cross Fell to the Tyne Gap, while the Helm Bar, a thin whirling cylinder of cloud, hovers from one to four miles away, marking the limit of the savage winds. When the Bar is black, rain will soon follow, but when it is white, the wind will blow with such frigid intensity that it can rip branches from trees, scorch tender young grass and reap a terrible harvest among new lambs. The Helm can be roaring down the fell-sides while there is a complete calm only a handful of miles away.

I stopped to commiserate with a farmer who was gap-walling despite the freezing wind. 'Aye, it's draughty, right enough,' he said, with typical upland understatement.

'Is this as bad as the wind gets?' I asked, watching my car rocking in the gusts.

'No, somedays it's fierce enough to blow the horns off a tup,' he said cheerily.

I headed back to the shelter of the car, battling to open the door against the wind. I had heard many tales about people and even horses and carts being blown over by the force of the Helm wind, and after experiencing it at first hand, I was more inclined to believe them. Cross Fell was once known as Fiends

Fell, because of the terrifying scream of the wind howling down the slopes, but St Paulinus exorcized the demons and placed a cross on the summit, earning it a change of name.

I reached Dufton and stopped to look at the handsome fountain on the green, erected by the London Lead Company, who operated the Dufton mine from the eighteenth century. Though ruthless in its treatment of workers who failed to toe the company line in the matter of church attendance or the demon drink, the Quaker-owned company's paternal concern for its workforce extended to the provision of decent housing and sanitation. The elaborate fountain commemorates the piped water supply provided for the village.

Full of justifiable pride, the company had a Latin inscription placed on the fountain which claims:

> Here is a clear fountain
> Shining with silver water.
> Shepherds do not defile it,
> Nor she-goats grazing on the mountain,
> Nor other herd or flock.
> No flying thing nor wild animal molests it,
> Nor branch fallen from tree.

Since the London Lead Company presumably used pipes made from its own product to carry the water to the fountain, their confidence in its purity may have been a little misplaced, but compared to the normal practice of collecting drinking water from the nearest stream, it was a considerable improvement.

Not all the company's activities were so beneficial to the water supply. The practice of 'hushing', damming water above a suspected source of lead ore and then releasing it suddenly to strip way the surface soil and rock, was so injurious that it was banned in 1811, after the Eden became so polluted that even the waters of the Solway Firth, forty miles away, were stained and thousands of fish were poisoned.

I drove on past more of the grey, gaunt villages, guarding the border marches of Eden, the Pennines spilling down behind them like a grass-covered glacier, poised to engulf them. Though the Scots raiders are long gone, there still seemed a faint air of menace hanging over the lonely villages and the long empty roads between them, but perhaps that was just the effect of the Helm wind on my already over-worked imagination.

My feelings of apprehension increased as I followed the road from Hilton which cuts across the corner of the army ranges, where I had recently faced a tank and lived to tell the tale. The road was open, for the army were not shooting that day, and I drove through a strange landscape littered with observation towers and the rusted, burnt-out hulks of tanks, which had been used as targets. In the middle of the ranges was a replica of a Belfast apartment block, a bizarre sight perched on an Eden hilltop. More soothing to my nerves was the sight of a farmer ploughing a field just outside the ranges, seagulls circling and drifting down to the freshly turned earth like dandelion seeds.

I spent the evening in Penrith, sampling the delights of what used to be one of the more unusual pubs of this or any region, the Agricultural Hotel. Any pub in the 1980s which still had a picture of Winston Churchill hanging on the wall and some table lamps made from the feet of dead deer on the mantelpiece, had to have something going for it, though what, I was never quite sure. It has always acted as the local for the auction mart, indeed a door connects them, and it was run for many years by a particularly crusty character, who served a few regulars and scowled at all visitors, but had some interesting and entertaining tales to tell if you could prize them out of him.

Like the previous owner, the portrait of Winston Church- ill and the deers' feet lamps are now gone, and the pub has been spruced up to attract a new breed of customers. However, I did find one throw-back, an old slaughterman who remem- bered the great days for the mart and the pub, the pedigree Shorthorn cattle sales that brought buyers pouring into Penrith from all over the country. 'Drovers would bring the cattle in along the old tracks from maybe fifty miles around. They'd

make a few bob extra charging the farmers to preen their beasts
before the sale, scraping and polishing the horns and brushing
the mud out of their coats and the like. The town was that full
that people would be sleeping on the floors, even in the mart.'

I had been intrigued by a story told by the old landlord and
related by the local newspaper. 'I heard about a farm down
where the Eden and Eamont meet, where there was an echo
that came across the water that used to drive the cattle mad. Do
you remember anything about that?'

'Oh aye, they were bad buggers, them. It would be
frustration, I suppose. They'd moo and the echo would moo
right back at them. None of us used to like dealing with those
beasts when they came in, they were that wild, you couldn't
handle them.'

I had been in the Agricultural Hotel one evening several
years before when a slaughterman wandered in and suddenly
whopped a severed bull's penis down on the bar, saying,
'Anybody who can beat that can have a fiver.' A couple of
people nearly fainted, though I'm not sure if it was revulsion or
excitement. I asked my companion if that was standard
slaughterhouse humour.

'Well it would just be a bit of a joke, like. Maybe it doesn't
do any harm to remind people once in a while where their meat
comes from. It doesn't grow up, ready jointed, wrapped and
frozen, you know, but they'd just as soon forget about that,
wouldn't they? We do the dirty work for them and then they
look down their noses at us for doing it.'

It was not a point of view I could argue against. We
chatted on for an hour or so on blander topics, then I steered a
slightly unsteady course towards my lodgings for the night. As I
walked down the street, I felt a warm southwesterly breeze on
my cheek; the Helm wind had relented.

# 14

# KIRKOSWALD AND NUNNERY WALKS

Nunnery Walks

back towards the fells, rejoining the Eden at the bridge just north of Lazonby. I left my car there and walked the lane to Kirkoswald, turning off to the church, tucked under the hill on which its tower stands. It is an unusual, perhaps unique arrangement, for church and tower are separated from each other by a distance of a hundred yards. The church is at the foot of the hill, the tower on its summit, enabling everyone working in the fields around to hear the church bell. While a call to worship was no doubt an important matter, a more vital function would certainly have been to warn the inhabitants of the approach of Scots raiders. To miss the call to divine worship might risk eternal damnation in the hereafter, but to fail to hear a warning of a Scots raiding party would almost certainly guarantee the swift onset of the hereafter.

In one corner of the graveyard, a yew hedge topiaried into battlements encircles the graves of Sir Timothy Fetherston-haugh and his second wife Bronwen. Even in death the local lord of the manor took care to keep himself aloof from his fellows. For the last four hundred years, the Fetherstonhaughs have ruled the Kirkoswald roost from a fine, rambling old mansion across the road from the church. It was originally a fourteenth-century pele tower, and later a seminary, which explains its name – the College – though the only educational process carried out there since the sixteenth century has been that of instructing the Fetherstonhaugh heirs in their rights and responsibilities.

The Fetherstonhaugh name looked immediately suspect to me, one of those linguistic pits the English upper-class delight in digging to trap foreigners, oiks, tradesmen and other lower orders. The classic of the genre is of course Cholmondeley, pronounced 'Chumley'. I had once owned a cat which I christened Chalfontstgilesbury, pronounced 'Cheeseby', however, so the Fetherstonhaughs certainly were not fooling me. I had them marked down as 'Fanshawes' as soon as I saw the inscription on the tombstone.

At the side of the church, I found St Oswald's Well. A metal cup on a chain lay by the iron lid covering Oswald's personal water supply and, ever the intrepid researcher, whatever the personal cost, I lowered the cup into the well, hauled it up and drank. To my relief and pleasure, the water was cool, clear and pure.

I left the church and walked up the village street, marvelling that such a tiny place could support three pubs, one, inevitably, named the Fetherstonhaugh Arms. The village is so ridiculously pretty and so perfectly manicured that it appears like a refugee from the Cotswolds, strangely dislocated in its Cumbrian setting. It is a frequent winner of that rural stand-by, the best-kept village competition, and is so immaculate that I felt a perverse and overwhelming urge to see it defiled with a MacDonalds franchise or a monstrous mound of pig muck in the middle of the street.

Such a pristine village made me suspect that it was far advanced in the process of fossilization, evident in the Home Counties, the Cotswolds and in whole swathes of English countryside, overwhelmed by the grey-haired shock troops of the pension brigades. No one likes to see heaps of rubbish and litter lying about, but a bit of clutter is a sign that there is work in progress, just like the detritus that accumulates around a farm. Villages without blots on their escutcheons suggest that, for the majority of the inhabitants, the day-to-day drudgery of earning a living is behind them, leaving them with nothing to do but manicure their gardens and complain about noise, traffic, litter, council services, rate bills, dogs fouling the footpaths, the need for a by-pass, the weather, the neighbours, the lack of good daily help, creeping bolshevism, moral degeneracy, the failure of certain persons to do their share of church brass polishing and all the other myriad obsessions of the genteel retired.

Once they would have remained in their original communities, finding a continuing role in family life. Now their increasing affluence and life expectancy, coupled with the erosion of family and community ties, encourage them to uproot themselves and make a new start in a tranquil rural area, suburbia taking a long lease on arcadia. While musing on this, I reached the top of Kirkoswald's idyllic village street, where I passed a little girl with a ghetto-blaster going full bore. She will have to go. . . .

I left the road and followed a footpath through the Eden prairies, big, wide-open fields, with most of the old hedges grubbed out, towards the tiny, impossibly pretty hamlet of Staffield. A mile along another quiet lane was Nunnery, and though I had scarcely walked a couple of miles so far and had a long way to go to reach my day's destination, I took time out to follow the Nunnery Walks by Croglin Water, which had once caused Wordsworth to launch into his customary raptures.

'Stop complaining, Dorothy, the rucksack isn't that heavy, and you only have to carry me over the muddy bits. Now quickly, out with your paper and pen, and get this down:

> Down from the Pennine Alps, how fiercely sweeps
> Croglin, the stately Eden's tributary!

The Benedictine nunnery which once stood on the site disappeared in Henry VIII's Dissolution of the Monasteries. In its place is a Georgian house, presiding over the entrance to the Nunnery Walks and admitting guests for bed and breakfast at the front, while dispensing ice cream from a side door.

The walks skirt a steep, thickly wooded ravine with Croglin Water tumbling over a series of falls on its way down to join the Eden. The heady smell of pine resin hung in the air as I followed the path down Croglin Water and downstream along the Eden for a mile or so. The green waters were flecked with white foam as the river tumbled into a gorge, beneath a high sandstone cliff.

Across the river, half-shrouded by the trees, is Sampson's Cave, not named for the hairless one, but for a murderer of that ilk. The construction of the Settle–Carlisle line north of Lazonby required a huge workforce to build the three major viaducts and three tunnels. As in the construction camps elsewhere on the line, drunkenness and brawling were by no means unknown and one brawl ended in death. The murderer hid in the cave now named after him, but was eventually captured, taken to Carlisle and hanged.

As I retraced my steps along the bank I passed two spry, white-haired old men, one carrying several gleaming fish suspended from a carrying rod. They were scanning the river with feverish intensity and passed me without a word or a glance. Not for the first time, I pondered the appeal of angling, not for the first time without success. My idea of a good day's fishing is ten seconds' work with a bag of lime or a stick of dynamite, ten minutes' work picking up the fish and ten hours spent lying on my back watching the clouds go by. The idea of fumbling with maggots, dry flies, waders and all the other paraphernalia which seems to be necessary and then spending several hours up to my armpits in an icy river, waving a rod to and fro, strikes me as less than the ideal way to spend a day.

I left the two anglers to their sport, if such it be, and climbed up the ravine alongside Croglin Water. I had the feeling of being back at the birth of the Eden, by the rocky gorge and foaming beck at Hell Gill. A path led off to a summer house and the ruins of a small, circular cell, in which mystics and Nunnery penitents would have meditated on the meaning of life, while a majestic waterfall crashed over the cliff nearby.

The Croglin waters flow down from the eponymous fell-side village, where Bram Stoker heard a vampire legend which inspired him to write *Dracula*. A Croglin girl was attacked in her room one summer night, by a creature that had 'a hideous brown face, with flaming eyes'. It bit her throat but fled when she screamed. Her brothers mounted guard and when it reappeared outside her window, one of them shot it in the leg. It fled into a family vault in the churchyard. The next morning they opened the vault and found the contents of the coffins mangled and strewn all over the ground. Only one coffin was intact, and when it was opened they found a brown, withered, mummified figure, with a fresh wound in its leg.

The nearby village of Renwick also has a legend of a huge bat that flew out of the church when it was being rebuilt in the eighteenth century, so Stoker had all the necessary source material to hand. He may have acquired just as much inspiration by walking the banks of Croglin Water as the sun went down, for the black midges, actually mosquitoes, which emerge in stinging hordes at dusk can drive even strong men to distraction with their biting, blood-sucking attacks. Half an hour by the upper Eden or one of its tributaries on a humid summer evening would have even the most sceptical writer reaching for the garlic.

Although the actual Benedictine nunnery has gone without trace, an unusual remnant still stands nearby, in a field below Cross House. Like the iron ring hanging from the mouth of the grotesque face on the door of Durham Cathedral, which guaranteed sanctuary to criminals who could lay a hand on it before their pursuers caught them, the Sanctuary Stone, inscribed with the word 'Sanctuarium', offered safe refuge to criminals. Though the sanctuary saved them from the more extreme rigours of medieval justice, the criminals did not escape scot-free, for they were escorted to a seaport and banished from the country for ever.

The stone cross has been restored and completely rebuilt, another of the pillars that seemed to mark my journey through Eden like milestones. The inscribed stone set into it is genuine enough, but the date, 1088, was probably carved at the behest of nuns anxious to prove the great antiquity of their foundation, without too much supporting evidence.

I walked on through a landscape where distinctions between rock, wood and earth were blurred by the softness of the Eden stone and the moist fertility of the Eden climate.

Drystone walls seemed to grow out of the earth, while moss, lichen and vegetation cloaked every outline. Ivy grew like a hedge, almost burying a wall. Tree stumps in a field stood like boulders, while one silhouetted on the skyline had the look of a pile of rotting masonry, crumbling slowly back into the earth.

I followed a quiet country lane around the shoulder of the hills, the course of the Eden below the forested Coombs detectable only by the sinuous path of the deciduous trees lining its banks, a ribbon of brighter green amongst the ranks of conifers. I left the lane for a forest track. The fresh breeze lost itself in the trees, leaving the forest still and quiet, the only sounds being birdsong and the wind soughing over the tree tops, while the sunlight trickled down through the branches. Lower on the slopes, the forest grew thicker and darker, with little light filtering between trunks as closely spaced as the stone pillars in a Romanesque church, the tussocks of pine needles between them like church kneelers.

I walked on through an avenue of gorse and came out of the forest into birch woods. The river tumbled over a weir, built before 1780 and destroyed in a flood in 1850. In the words of a contemporary writer, 'when the river is swollen, the sullen murmur of this cascade is awfully tremendous and causes a tremulous shuddering in the ground'. Even now, in its ruined state, it is an impressive sight. I stood spellbound for a moment, gazing at the delicate tracery of the birches against a deep blue sky. Natural beauty swiftly lost a battle with lunch, however, and I followed the river to Armathwaite.

I stood on the bridge for a few minutes, watching the broad sweep of the Eden and the small green rowing boats dotting its surface, as anglers probed the cool, shaded waters beneath the trees. It was to be my last crossing of the river; from here to the end of Eden on the Solway Firth the river would lie between me and the colder, wilder lands to the north and west.

# 15
# ARMATHWAITE
# TO
# WETHERAL

river Eden near Armathwaite

Sowerby, Little Salkeld and Lazonby, I had finally timed an arrival correctly, reaching the Duke's Head at the far side of the bridge well before closing time. I rewarded myself with a large lunch and several cups of coffee in the Last Cast bar, surrounded by brass powder flasks, fishing reels and hunting horns, though neither I nor the other customers appeared to be huntin', shootin' and fishin' types.

I left the pub and followed a lane parallel to the Eden, past a line of tall tree stumps like standing stones, an elongated row of Long Meg's Daughters running down towards the river. The line of the Pennines was receding and shrinking in the distance to the north, almost obscured by the low hills closer to the river, becoming just a grey-tinted memory of Defoe's wall of brass, fading into the afternoon haze.

I turned off the lane to rejoin the banks of the Eden, the river dividing around a long island. The path was carpeted with wildflowers and the river lapped as rhythmically at the bank as waves against a shore. Two oystercatchers stood like self-important aldermen on a rock in the river and a pair of swans drifted in the current by the far bank. Wooden anglers' huts punctuated the riverbank like milecastles on Hadrian's Wall. Rowing boats were also tethered to the bank at regular intervals, and I felt a strong temptation to liberate one and just drift down river with the stream. It was a temptation I resisted, partly because of my strong sense of personal morality but, more importantly, because they all appeared to be padlocked to their moorings.

I walked across a stretch of golden sand, a beach on the

river, and my footprints were the only marks on its pristine surface. It was an idyllic scene, the beach, the thickly-wooded slopes and the afternoon sunlight slanting down through the trees, sparkling on the surface of the river.

The river flowed on into a gorge ahead, compressed between the faces of Eden Brows. Flood debris festooned the branches eight, even ten feet above the waterline. From a valley so wide that the word had almost ceased to be adequate to describe it, the Eden was now again running through a genuine river valley, back in its private world, while I patrolled the no-man's-land between the river and the woods.

The railway ran along the top of the steep bank above the river, its last contact before swinging away to begin the run into Carlisle. It had run close by throughout Eden, the river naturally finding the line of least resistance, the railway engineers following closely in its tracks and drawing water from it for their steam engines, in those pre-diesel days. I came across an iron pillar, stamped with MR for the Midland Railway, amongst the undergrowth. It probably marked the line of a water extraction pipe, but it looked like the key from a giant clockwork railway set.

A lone Friesian cow was playing queen of the castle on an island in the middle of the river, perhaps waiting for a drought so that she could return to the mainland. An angler stood in the shallows, immobile as a heron. The shadows were lengthening and the wind swinging into the north carried the first cold hint of winter. I passed a mound of mysterious moss-encrusted stones, surrounded by the skeletons of dead elm trees, strips of bark hanging from them like shreds of skin. In a huge rookery nearby, the rooks were gathering, like monks for vespers, as the sun sank low in the sky.

In a corner of the wood was a solitary tombstone, encrusted with lichen and moss. It was erected in memory of Matthew Knublay and his wife Mary, who died in 1814 and 1822. It was an oddly moving sight, alone in the dark woodland by the river. I wondered if the heap of stones back in the wood had once been a church, abandoned to the encroaching Eden, or if the Knublays' last resting-place lay outside consecrated grounds because of some crime or heresy, but there were no answers to be found among the trees and I walked on.

I quickened my pace as journey's end, for this day at least, came into view, a beautiful long stretch of the Eden, framing Corby Castle on a bluff above the water. Another set of caves, carved from the rock, stood high above the near bank of the river, but these three linked caves are genuinely old, and may have been the inspiration for Lacy's Caves. They are walled at the front, with narrow embrasures giving on to the river, and were used as hermitages, a legend claiming that St Constantine once occupied them.

In the rockface nearby are inscriptions carved by William Mounsey, who travelled the Eden from sea to source in 1850, pausing to carve Greek and Latin inscriptions and inaccurate quotations from Walton's *The Compleat Angler* on the Eden stone along the way. When he reached Black Fell Moss, he had a pillar set up, known locally as the 'Jew Stone', because of the Star of David incised in it.

On one side, in Greek, was carved:

Seek the river of the soul – whence it springs, and when thou hast served the body in a certain order – when thou hast acknowledged thy duty to the sacred Scriptures – thou shalt be raised again to the order from which thou art fallen.

Below it, again in Greek, was the inscription:

Let us flee with ships to our dear native land; for we have a country from which we have come and our Father is there.

On the other side, in mimicry of a Roman altar dedicated to the gods of the river, is the Latin inscription:

William Mounsey, a lone traveller, having commenced his journey at the mouth and finished it at the source, fulfilled his vow to the Genius and nymphs of the Eden on the 15th March 1850.

Unfortunately for Mounsey, the workers building the Settle–Carlisle line did not share his classical education, and when a group of them came across the pillar, they did what any group of red-blooded Englishmen, faced with a stone inscribed in a foreign language, would do – they smashed it to pieces.

After lying in fragments for a century, it was rescued from the fells, appropriately enough by the local fell rescue organization, who brought the pieces down on a stretcher as a training exercise. The Jew Stone now lies in a barn in Mallerstang, awaiting restoration.

I walked on towards Wetheral, across the river from Corby Castle, a handsome edifice with a stone lion on its roof and a remarkable collection of eighteenth-century follies in its garden. Two grottoes look out across the Eden at water level, and alongside, a flight of steps leads up from the river to a statue of Nelson standing in the middle of a small pond, something of an indignity for the great sailor. Above are a series of Italianate cascades, topped by a temple carved with mermaids, Neptune and a lion.

The water issues from a grotesque head, with the hounds of Hades at either side, but it may need the earthly ministrations of a plumber, for the flow of water is down to a mere trickle. Elsewhere in the grounds are a dovecote disguised as a classical temple and a classical tempietto. In Corby itself, the village smithy was reconstructed to represent Vulcan's Forge, with a classical porch under which the horses were shod. Pevsner hated it, but others have been kinder.

The viaduct of the Newcastle–Carlisle railway spans the Eden ahead, but I turned up the hill away from the river, into the Hampstead of Eden, Wetheral. Large houses, an immaculately tailored green, an hotel, an expensive restaurant, even a conference centre, sum up the village. It is quiet all day and comes to life when the Carlisle commuters return at dusk, descending on their roosts like rooks. On summer weekends the air is rich with the murmur of a hundred lawnmowers and hosepipes.

The village has a pub as well, but it was not yet open; I

could only seem to manage to get one right a day. In such an affluent enclave there seemed no point in even trying to find someone interested in making a few pounds by driving me down to Lazonby, and I telephoned for a taxi from Carlisle, then sat on a wall, enjoying the last of the sunshine. When my taxi arrived, I had to explain how to get to Lazonby, not because the driver did not know where it was, but because, in his classic country phrase, 'If I was going there, I wouldn't start from here.'

# 16 CARLISLE

Carlisle Castle

December day as grey and cold as the one on which I had begun my journey twelve months before. All that separated me from journey's end on the shore of the Solway was a few more miles of river and the city of Carlisle.

I cannot imagine that even Carlisle's best friends find it an attractive place. The centuries of incessant warfare and raiding by Scots, moss-troopers and border reivers have left Carlisle pinched and grim-faced, its buildings huddled in the lee of the castle, like children hiding behind their mother's skirts, still anxiously peering towards the north.

Separated from Carlisle by a dual carriageway, the stranded castle glowers defiantly down on the city, its gaunt keep set within the walls like a decaying tooth in a socket. The Eden stone looks warm in the walls of rural farmhouses, glowing the colour of ripe, red gooseberries in the rays of the setting sun, but that same red light from the western skies seems to stain the walls of this cold, unforgiving castle like blood.

The air of foreboding was heightened by the grey, raw day, the wind howling round me as I entered the castle. The gatehouse, the only break in the monumental walls, was once protected by a drawbridge, a barbican, oak gates, a portcullis and a pair of stout oak doors, evidence, if any were needed, of Eden's war-torn past. No ruler, whether Roman, Anglo-Saxon, Scottish, Norman or English, could ever feel really secure in his hold on this far-off, disputed land, its allegiance as shifting and unpredictable as the sands of the Solway.

Even before the Romans finally abandoned Britain in the

178

fifth century, they had given up the attempt to hold the frontier at Hadrian's Wall and had retreated to Stainmore, leaving Eden to the mercy of the invaders from the north, described by the historian Gildas: 'Foul hordes of Picts and Scots, like tawny worms coming forth in the burning heat of noon out of the deepest recesses of their holes, hastily land from their curraghs . . . differing in manners, but all sharing the same thirst for blood, and more eager to shroud their villainous faces with beards than to cover with decent clothing those parts of their bodies which required it.' Even as early as the fifth century, true Scotsmen obviously wore nothing beneath their kilts.

Though the Scots and the English were the principal architects of Eden's thousand years of misery, the Danes made their mark too. In the late ninth century they destroyed Carlisle completely, burning the town, demolishing the walls and killing every man, woman and child. So complete was the destruction that grass and oak trees grew over the ruins in the following century.

In 1092, William Rufus took Carlisle and fortified it. Although it remained nominally part of England from that time on, the city was by no means spared the attentions of the Scots. In 1138 Malcolm of Scotland raided with an army down the Eden Valley, where, according to the *Chronicle of Lanercost*, 'the whole land was laid waste and no rank or age and neither sex was spared'. Men and children were killed, women taken into slavery, to be driven north with the Scots' booty of sheep, cattle, goods and valuables.

Henry II retook Carlisle and granted the city its first charter. He also created Inglewood, one of the largest forests in England, to the south of Carlisle. Though much of it was wooded, 'forest' referred to an area set aside for the king's hunting. The Forest Laws were strict and savage; tree-felling, clearing the undergrowth and disturbing the ground by pro-specting for minerals were all forbidden, and hunting was reserved for the king and his cronies.

Part of the appeal of the legend of Robin Hood no doubt sprang from his defiance of the hated Forest Laws, and

Inglewood Forest had its own band of merrie men – Willyam of Cloudesley, Adam Bell and Clym of the Clough. A ballad commemorated their exploits, which included Willyam, 'an archer good ynough', splitting a hazel wand with an arrow and shooting an apple off his son's head (any resemblance to any other legends, living or dead, is entirely coincidental). The medieval fascination with Arthurian legend and chivalry led to a whole string of romances about Inglewood and 'Merrie Carlisle', where Chretien de Troyes claimed Arthur's court had been sited.

In reality the city remained far from 'merrie'. The border between England and Scotland was undefined, and the marsh, moorland and forest to the north of Carlisle, known as the 'Debatable Land', was crossed by tracks used only by smugglers, raiders and invading armies. It was the preserve of rievers and moss-troopers, who raided, stole, burned and killed to north and south of their territory, with equal indifference and impunity. The succeeding centuries saw little change, the Scots and English continually battling for control of Carlisle, the north of Eden a wild, lawless territory. The people hid within the shielding city walls, and few were brave or foolish enough to build outside their protection.

The organized warfare reached its peak in the reign of Edward I, 'responsible for the inflaming of more hatred in these Border lands than any other single individual'. The route taken by his armies on their annual invasions into Scotland could be traced from the corpses of Scots men, women and children and the smoke from burning buildings. Even in his death throes, Edward was still trying to force his sick and wasted body north for one last assault. He died in 1307 on the Solway shore, where a stone monument commemorates him, but a more appropriate site would be the slaughterhouse or the cemetery, for, if his campaigns brought him glory, they left only a legacy of blood and bodies behind.

Even after the end of the centuries of war that Edward did much to inspire, the border raiding continued, while the Civil War produced even greater torment, including the longest siege in Carlisle's history. The castle held out for eight months before capitulating. Horses were kept alive with thatch from the houses, before being eaten by the starving inhabitants, who also fed on hemp seed, dogs and rats. Two years after the siege, in 1647, Carlisle was described as 'a model of misery and desolation as the sword, famine and plague had left it'.

Carlisle avoided more than passing involvement in the Jacobite rebellion of 1715, but the '45 found the city once more at the forefront, and once more besieged. General Wade was powerless to intervene, stranded in Newcastle by the appalling state of the roads, and Prince Charles Edward – Bonnie Prince Charlie – was able to lay siege successfully to the virtually undefended city, entering Carlisle to be proclaimed King James III.

His reign was a brief one. He marched south on 22 November and returned on 19 December, after a heavy defeat on Clifton Moor, near Penrith, leaving many of his followers buried in a mass grave. He fled north, while his rearguard delayed the pursuing Duke of Cumberland, who retook the city on 30 December, capturing hundreds of the rebels and incarcerating them in the castle's dungeons. Three hundred were crammed into a single cell, fighting to reach the air from the narrow window slit. In the morning, the dead lay everywhere, trampled to death by the survivors. So many rebels had been captured that they drew lots to decide their fate. One in twenty was tried, the others were transported. They were the fortunate ones, for those that stood trial had only one fate, the gallows.

Among the hanged was MacDonald of Keppoch, the prototype of Scott's Fergus MacIvor in *Waverley*. By a cruel irony, the tiny window high in his cell, the only break in the keep's featureless north wall, afforded MacDonald a tantalizing view out across the Eden towards Scotland. The stone of the window sill – the same soft stone as Lacy's caves – is grooved an inch deep, worn by the hands of Scots prisoners clinging to the sill, as they strained for a glimpse of the land beyond the Eden, to which they would never return.

The dungeons in the keep and the squalid cell beneath the castle gatehouse, a dank, cold hole in the ground, into which prisoners were lowered through a trap-door, are scarcely cheering sights even today, but what brought the suffering of those wretched prisoners into vivid focus for me, was not so much the actual places of their confinement, but the symbols of their humanity, the graffiti carved in the wall of MacDonald's cell and those pitiful indentations in the window sill. Yet even those haunting sights paled beside the unforgettable human traces in the lower dungeons of the keep.

The cold within the keep strikes to the bone. The thick stone walls are solid, ugly and impregnable, perforated only by thin slits. Electric light now illuminates the rooms, but a claustrophobic spiral staircase in the wall still has the atmosphere of the dark past and caused in me a flicker of apprehension.

Brightly lit, the dungeons seem stripped of any residual menace, until the scars on the walls begin to tell their tale. A narrow stone ledge runs around the foot of the walls, a few inches above the floor, where the prisoners would sit or stand, and the holes where their manacles were fixed are still clearly visible. In the far wall of the end dungeon is an initially baffling sight, a stone darker than those around it, cool and moist to the touch and worn into strange, smooth depressions, like a rock in the bed of the Eden.

I defy even the most world-weary cynic to look on that stone without being moved, for those depressions were worn by prisoners, over hundreds of years, pressing their parched tongues to the stone to extract a little precious moisture. This 'Licking Stone' was always wet and in times of heavy rain it would drip water. Twenty or so years ago, repairs to the fabric of the building somehow disrupted the flow of water through the stone, but it remains damp and cold even now, mute testimony to past suffering. The chill that I felt looking at that cold stone had little to do with the December day.

After that grim scene, I needed some air. I climbed up on to the battlements, where two cannon still point defiantly towards Scotland, though they now overlook a tranquil scene: a children's playground, tennis courts and a park.

Walking back towards the Eden, I turned for a last look at the castle before following the river out towards the Solway. From the north, the castle presented an almost completely featureless mask, the blank stone face of the keep broken only by MacDonald's window, opening like an eye socket in a skull.

# 17
# THE SOLWAY FIRTH

Edward I Monument

THE EDEN FLOWS WIDE, DEEP

and slow as it skirts Carlisle, keeping a wary distance from the castle, the city and the industrial area to the west. Carlisle's euphoria at the ending of centuries of warfare was short-lived. The rapid industrialization of the city was followed by a time of terrible poverty, with hunger riots and weavers in the textile industry even petitioning the Regent to 'send us all to America'. William Farish's nineteenth-century autobiography speaks of the times when 'it was no uncommon thing for our house to be without bread for weeks together; and I cannot remember to have ever seen, in my very early years, a joint of meat of any kind on my father's table'.

The city also suffered all the horrors that afflicted the other industrial cities of Britain in those halcyon Victorian days: typhus and cholera epidemics, poverty, hunger and deprivation which left the majority of the population with 'pinched pale faces, many scarred with smallpox, many bearing the seal of death by early decline'.

The stench and filth of the streets shocked the Carlisle Relief Committee, which could 'hardly find words to express the amount of filth, or to depict the abominable nuisances existing'. The stink of industry and sewage now borne on the wind brought the committee's words back to me, though the prime sources of the smell, a sewage treatment plant and a tyre factory, would have passed unnoticed amid the stench of the nineteenth-century streets.

The remains of the old power station on the banks of the Eden had recently been demolished, leaving an empty industrial plain on which bulldozers and heavy lorries were performing their ponderous, deafening rituals. The river was modestly screened by a thin belt of birch and conifers from this industrial dereliction close at hand. It is to be the site of a business park, and future travellers will no doubt see gleaming, hi-tech buildings in carefully landscaped grounds. I saw only mud, sludge, twisted metal, sewage pans and electricity pylons – truly the end of Eden.

The north bank of the river, uncontaminated by Carlisle industry, had already returned to open country, the transition marked by one of the recurring images of my journey through Eden, a rusting, abandoned car, perched on the bank, just above the water line. River floods had filled it with silt to the level of the bottom of the windows, and a carpet of grass lined the inside and spilled out across the bonnet and boot.

An army of pylons marched away into the distance, four separate ranks crossing the river within a hundred yards, seeming to patrol the last frontier of urban Carlisle. The industrial interlude had been mercifully brief. Over the river, another familiar rural landmark reappeared, and, after such frequent acquaintance along the length of Eden, I greeted the mounds of black-bagged 'big bales' like old friends.

I passed under the stone bridge of a disused railway, the last bridge across the Eden, and fought my way along a less than well-used path, jabbed by gorse and whipped about the ears by thorn branches for my impertinence. Resolving to add a machete to a Hiking Boot's list of essential supplies, I abandoned the path for the field alongside, reassured by the well-worn track that I was not the first to admit defeat. Cloud was piling up in the north-west, but here by the Eden, the pale sunlight still shone on the bleached stalks of the dead grass. The last of Carlisle's housing estates curled away to the south, and Eden returned to a state of grace, marked by a pure white swan, drifting in the current near the far bank.

I walked on through a narrow pasture between the river and the skeleton of the Solway railway and into rough wood-land. Having survived the thorns assaulting my head, I now faced trial by brambles intent on savaging my legs. Every few yards I was brought to a juddering halt as a thick stem wrapped itself around my shins, before, inevitably, one caught my ankle, sending me plunging headlong into a dense bramble patch and curing me of a lifelong fondness for blackberries in an instant.

As the Eden curved sharply away to the north, I left the bank, not without some relief after the thorny assaults of the last mile, and walked up to Grinsdale through a patch of primordially boggy ground. All the inhabitants of the tiny village must have been occupied in their post-prandial siestas, for even the farm dogs failed to bark as I walked down the main street and followed the old green lane to the church.

A huge beech tree guards the entrance to the churchyard, its trunk twisted on itself like a braided rope. The church, St Kentigern's, is locked, 'because of its exposed position' according to a notice on the door. Firing slits in the side of the tower suggest that it has always been dangerously exposed. I peered through the windows at its plain interior, then rejoined the river bank among the flood debris. Driftwood, bottles, plastic, even a supermarket trolley had somehow managed to find its way down here, resting in the shallows before resuming an improbable journey to the sea.

Beyond the river are the floodlight towers of the vast Kingsmoor railway marshalling yard, the most up-to-date in Europe on its completion in 1963. It is ominously close to Cargo, an enormous munitions dump, which suggests that its scale and modernity may not be entirely connected with its civilian goods traffic.

The river had begun a series of huge sweeping curves which continue until it reaches the Solway, and the end of the freshwater Eden is near at hand, for beyond Beaumont, the next village, it becomes tidal. The closeness of the Solway marshes was obvious from the multitude of water and wading birds on and around the river. Half a dozen different breeds of duck rose from the surface, and a heron, like some prehistoric throwback, flapped lazily away.

On the bank, an oyster-catcher probed the soft earth with

its long, orange beak. In spring it would fly inland to nest on the pebbly beach of one of Eden's countless side-streams and rivers. A swan preened itself in the shallows by the far bank, and further on, another flight of duck wheeled up and away in their familiar figure of eight, passing high overhead, before dropping back on to the surface of the river behind me. Two ash trees stood together on the bank in curious disharmony, one without a single remaining seedpod, as bare as a whip, the other still smothered in clumps of seed, some trailing down into the river.

Though the last of Eden's towns now lay behind me, the next rubbish dump was never far away. The one I reached at the next bend of the river was one of the most comprehensive of the whole journey, containing everything up to and including a kitchen sink. The far bank, by contrast, looked a green and pleasant land, although its tranquillity was perhaps deceptive, for just over the brow of the hill is a vast, unexploded bomb, the Cargo munitions dump. It has been in use since the First World War, when problems of drunkenness in workers there, and at the nearby munitions factories around Gretna, led to a bizarre experiment in social engineering.

The Carlisle & District State Management Scheme was an attempt by the government to impose, if not temperance, at least moderation on its munitions workers. All the breweries and pubs in the area were taken over, many closed down, and those that remained were subjected to restricted opening hours and a rigorous code: no 'treating' (the buying of rounds); no people showing signs of intoxication to be served; no 'loose women' to be tolerated.

More positive measures included the building of new pubs and an emphasis on the provision of food, newspapers and recreations such as bowling. The results of this experiment by the teetotal Lloyd George were utterly predictable. The pubs were about as appealing to the Carlisle inhabitants as kissing their grannies, and the scheme's only lasting effect on the problems of drunkenness among the munitions workers was to make it far worse.

The evening shift from the Gretna munitions factories would board the last train to Carlisle, the nearest place where the pubs were still open, passing the hat round for a collection for the driver, payable if he got the train in ahead of schedule. The faster he went, the more he collected. The train would hurtle into Carlisle station, screech to a halt and a torrent of men would pour into the surrounding pubs, where ranks of glasses of beer and whisky would be awaiting them. In the twenty minutes or so available, the men would drink themselves close to oblivion and then spill out into the streets, swearing, brawling, harassing women and collapsing in the gutters, leaving the people of Carlisle to wonder how this could possibly be helping the war effort.

Though the State Management Scheme is over, the munitions linger on beneath the hill north of the river. Several years ago, a small earthquake hit Eden, its epicentre this area to the north of Carlisle. It shook the walls of my house a few miles to the south, but did no great damage, except to the nerves. Almost to a man, the initial reaction of the people that I spoke to had been the same as mine: that there had been an explosion at either Cargo or Windscale, now known as Sellafield and previously known as Calder Hall. (The name is changed every few years, but if a rose by any other name would smell as sweet, Calder Hall/Windscale/Sellafield, by whatever name the public relations department dream up for it next, will still hit my nostrils like a putrefying fish.)

I uttered a silent prayer that the loudest noise heard from Cargo or, indeed, Sellafield, in my own or anyone else's lifetime, would be the lowing of the cattle grazing on the hill, and turned my attention to the virtuoso displays by the diving ducks on the river, as they disappeared below the surface for what seemed like minutes at a time.

The breeze was strengthening steadily from the west, carrying a salt tang from the Solway marshes, as the river again swung away in a sweeping curve to the north. The level ground of the river bank widened to a lovely walk under a canopy of beech trees, before giving way to open water meadows. The marks of webbed feet were imprinted in the mud at the water's edge. I passed a battered old hut made of upended railway sleepers, roofed with corrugated metal and painted with tar. It provides some shelter for stock, but the fireplace suggests its principal use is for wild fowlers, anglers or water bailiffs.

The Eden is broken by a score of islets in the middle of the stream, perhaps the remnants of the bank when the river meandered closer to Rockcliffe. Now it takes a more direct course, slicing at the bank on which I was walking, with clumps of freshly fallen turf lying in the water swirling and bubbling beneath the bank. By scything away the banks, the river is reclaiming its own. This rich, alluvial soil was laid here by countless floods over thousands of years; what the river gives, in time, it also takes back.

The towers of the Kingsmoor floodlights still loomed beyond Cargo Hill, as the river bent back to the west towards Rockcliffe, the spire of the church contrasting with the secular, sinister, red brick tower of some military installation across the river. The narrow collar of land on which Rockcliffe stands was now all that separated the Eden from the Esk, and the proximity of the mudflats and marshes was emphasized by the duck, gulls and wading birds filling the air.

I reached a narrow gulley, where the water level was rising steadily, against the flow of the river, signalling that the Eden had now become tidal. I walked on over a wide expanse of water meadow, regularly inundated by high tides and floods, with any depression in the ground quickly filled with standing, brackish water.

There was a heavy splash as a big salmon broke surface on the river. In the sky high above, the vapour trails of jets, outward bound for America, counterpointed the flight patterns of geese and duck and the ragged formations of gulls passing overhead. Migrating birds in their millions rest and feed on the Solway shores, and in the autumn and spring the skies are full of long, trailing Vs of geese, honking softly to each other as they fade into the night.

As the river passed beneath Rockcliffe's steep red cliffs, I could look due west, where there was now no further land to be seen but the mudflats and marshes of the Solway. Pools and gulleys full of water lay everywhere, and duck were flighting off from all sides as I walked on across the meadows, a herd of cattle scattering before me, their hooves churning the soft ground. Ahead the river began to open up, broadening into a sheet of water and mudflats, its channel disappearing from sight beneath the tide flowing in from the west. The breeze strengthened off the Solway and the sky was awash with birds, their cries a constant sorrowful refrain, as they swooped low over the flat, empty land and skimmed the water.

Awash with birdlife, the Solway sees few humans. Once bustling and prosperous, Eden's north shore, like Eden itself, has slipped into torpor. Cattle still graze the sea-washed turf, but the huge herds trudging and swimming across the Solway, goaded on by their drovers, have long faded into history. Gone too are the salt pans on the Burgh sands, gone like the salt beef for the forces. The Port Carlisle canal was doubly abandoned; filled in and converted to a railway line, which itself was then closed; the great iron viaduct across the Firth long dismantled and now marked only by the stone piers on either shore.

Two boats a week once left Port Carlisle for Liverpool and Ireland. Others sailed for America with a human cargo of miners from the faltering West Cumbrian coal and iron workings and weavers from Carlisle's silent mills. Few boats now ply the Solway, though the haaf-netters still stand chest-deep in the in-rushing tide, their nets billowing behind them like deathwings for salmon blind-driven by the imperative to spawn and die in the becks and streams where Eden begins.

The Solway remains; a treacherous mixture of marshes and shifting sands with a tidal rip that can engulf the unwary. At low tide, its mudflats and broad, shallow river channels provide a means of crossing from England to Scotland; the name Solway derives from 'sul wath' – the 'muddy ford' across the Solway from Burgh-by-Sands. It was the main medieval route into Scotland and is usable today, though without expert local knowledge, only a fool would attempt it, for when the tide turns, the in-rush of water can be swift, ferocious and deadly.

I have walked along the Solway shore, looking out over the sands, with the Eden flowing gently by in its channel, and heard a quiet, but unusual sound. Within minutes, a wave of foam had flooded the sands, the Eden disappearing beneath a sheet of water, spreading from shore to shore. In winter storms, the tide comes in with a roar, a mass of foam at its head, sweeping up the Solway; it is not hard to see why so many lives have been lost here.

A seventh-century life of Adamnan, Abbot of Iona, described the tidal rush of the Solway as 'so rapid that if the best steed in Saxonland [England], ridden by the best horseman, were to start from the edge when the tide begins to flow, he could only bring his rider ashore by swimming, so extensive is the strand and so impetuous the tide'. Alexander II of Scotland discovered its full ferocity, when returning from a raid into Eden in 1216. His army set out across the Solway, but was caught by the tide, and, according to the *Chronicle of Lanercost*, 1,900 men were swept away to their deaths.

Although the river channel can still be identified at low water throughout the length of the Solway, there is no Eden Valley now. Here there are just the flat lands on either shore and ahead only the Solway leading on to the sea. The true end of Eden is here, where the river emerges from the lee of the Rockcliffe marshes and becomes more of the sea than of the land.

On the shore, standing like a marking post of Eden's end, is a stone monument. I turned down the muddy lane towards it, a lane worn deep by countless marching feet down the centuries; now only the boots of the tourists and the wheels of a farmer's tractor churn its surface into mud.

The sky was reddening into sunset as I reached the shore, and the sight of a flock of Swaledale sheep grazing the turf around the monument took my mind back to the start of my journey through Eden, at a rough stone pillar high on the fells, put there by a woman who had done nothing but good for Eden, using her wealth and power to benefit her people.

Like the person it commemorates, the monument to Edward I, a twenty-foot tower on a stepped plinth, its arched top capped by a stone cross, is on a far grander scale than the humble Lady Anne's Pillar on Black Fell Moss. It was built to honour a great English king, but, as with Edward himself, close scrutiny shows up its faults, for it leans drunkenly to one side, and presides only over an empire of marshland and brackish water.

I stood looking across the water towards the Lochmabenstane, a standing stone that marks the northern end of the ford, which was frequently used by Edward I on his slaughtering, pillaging expeditions. The hatred engendered by his obsessive warfare with Scotland far outlived him, but he also earned the grudging respect of one of his chief opponents, Robert de Brus. He declared that there was more glory in winning half a foot of land from Edward I than a whole kingdom from Edward II, and said he feared the old man's bones more than he did the living son.

From this desolate, wind-swept place, Edward I took his last look across to the land of the old enemy. He never made the final crossing, dying here on the shore of the Solway, weakened by old age and ravaged by dysentery: no glorious death for an English hero.

His monument, shielded from the curious and the malicious by a six-foot spiked iron fence, carries the inscription: 'Edwardi primi famam optimi Angliae regis'. This description of Edward I as the greatest English King sits uncomfortably on the shoulders of the 'Hammer of the Scots', begetter of the Hundred Years War with France and initiator of three hundred years of war with Scotland. If he was the greatest, God save us from the rest! Within a few feet of the monument, the line of the flood tide was marked by the tributes of the twentieth century to this paragon of seven hundred years ago: driftwood, plastic rubbish and an empty gin bottle.

I turned my back on that cold tombstone of past English power and might, walking away from the Solway and the Eden for the last time. At the top of the hill, as I entered the village of

Burgh-by-Sands, I passed a monument to English power and might on the threshold of the twenty-first century – a bungalow. Eden has spent a thousand years and more at the eye of great events; perhaps it has earned its quiet retirement at the margins of English life. After centuries of bloodshed and destruction in Eden, who would not prefer bungalow bliss in this earthly paradise?

# ·𝒫OSTSCRIPT·

ON the far shore of the Solway a handful of lights prick the December gloom. The bony finger of Edward's monument stands even more gaunt against a sky swollen with snow clouds. The setting sun gutters and is extinguished in the wasteland of water stretching out to the west. Birds and sheep fall silent as the first gritty flurries of snow sting the surface of the dying Eden, merging with the salt tide flowing in from the sea.

High on the fells by Eden's source, Ben Alderson has already deciphered the message in the dull red sky and turned back up the hill towards his sheep, striding past the rough stone pillar without a glance. His bootprint in the sodden peat fills slowly with Eden water, dripping constantly from a small overhang of peat.

# INDEX

# INDEX